C000144016

Story-writing
SCAFFOLDS

Written by
Christine Butterworth and Maria Roberts

Teachers' Resource Book

HOPSCOTCH
EDUCATIONAL PUBLISHING

Published by
Hopscotch Educational Publishing Ltd
Unit 2
The Old Brushworks
56 Pickwick Road
Corsham
Wiltshire
SN13 9BX
Tel: 01249 701701

© 2003 Hopscotch Educational Publishing
Reprinted 2005

Written by Christine Butterworth and Maria Roberts
Series design by Blade Communications
Cover illustration by Kirsty Wilson
Illustrated by Jane Bottomley

Printed and bound by Athenaeum Press, Gateshead

ISBN 1-904307-40-X

Christine Butterworth and Maria Roberts hereby
assert their moral right to be identified as the
authors of this work in accordance with the
Copyright, Designs and Patents Act, 1988.

All rights reserved. This book is sold subject to the
condition that it shall not, by way of trade or
otherwise, be lent, hired out or otherwise circulated
without the publisher's prior consent in any form of
binding or cover other than that in which it is
published and without a similar condition, including
this condition, being imposed upon the subsequent
purchaser.

No part of this publication may be reproduced, stored
in a retrieval system, or transmitted, in any form or
by any means, electronic, mechanical, photocopying,
recording or otherwise, without the prior permission
of the publisher, except where photocopying for
educational purposes within the school or other
educational establishment that has purchased this
book is expressly permitted in the text.

Every effort has been made to trace the owners of
copyright of material in this book and the publisher
apologises for any inadvertent omissions. Any
persons claiming copyright for any material should
contact the publisher who will be happy to pay the
permission fees agreed between them and who will
amend the information in this book on any
subsequent reprint.

Year 5

Story-writing
SCAFFOLDS

CONTENTS

INTRODUCTION

Story-writing Scaffolds for Year 5 is intended for use in schools to help teach children how to write effective short stories in a variety of different genres. It improves children's ability to organise their writing so that it has purpose by familiarising them with a system of planning stories which they can apply to any title. As they work through the units, the children assemble a portfolio of stories containing genre-specific vocabulary and writing features. The chosen text types correspond with those in the Framework's text-level objectives for each half-term.

Each unit also includes information and activities on at least one sentence-level objective. Thus the book also enhances the children's knowledge of grammar, their punctuation and style.

THE PROGRAMME CONTAINS:

a teachers' book comprising:

- notes for teachers on the genres
- copies of exemplar stories together with teaching notes
- guidance on how to develop grammar skills in children's writing
- guidance on how to help children write in the particular genre

a resource book of photocopiable material comprising:

- illustrated versions of the exemplar stories especially produced for children
- notes for the children on understanding the grammar (optional reference material)
- photocopiable activity sheets to reinforce the grammar (optional)
- notes and tips for the children on writing stories (optional reference material)
- differentiated story scaffolds which enable them to choose the course of the story they are about to write
- vocabulary banks for them to use and add to.

HOW TO USE THE PROGRAMME

1 After examining examples of stories in the target genre by established writers, read and discuss the exemplar story with the children, using the notes in the margin to highlight the examples of the unit's grammatical teaching point and writing feature. The children should follow the story using their own illustrated version from the Resource book.

2 Next read through and explain the 'Understanding the grammar and punctuation' section of the unit. The children can do the activities orally together or independently on paper.

3 Then explain the 'Helpful hints' and 'Writing features' sections of the unit to the children.

4 Read through the story scaffolds with the children. Then give them the differentiated word banks and ask them to record their own vocabulary suggestions in the space provided.

Give the children time to plan, write and edit their stories. Each child can then store the best copies of their stories in a writing folder.

NOTES FROM THE AUTHORS

The activities in each unit, from reading the model story to composing a story using the scaffolds, can be used in shared or guided time, with the children working collaboratively or individually.

The order of activities for each unit corresponds exactly with the sequence for the teaching of writing outlined in *Grammar for Writing* (DfEE 0107/2000). First the model story can be discussed and its grammatical and thematic features interrogated during shared reading. Next the grammar and punctuation activities can be undertaken to reinforce the children's understanding of the relevant sentence-level objectives. The helpful hints section, story scaffolds and vocabulary banks support the teacher and children in shared writing sessions and in subsequent guided and independent writing.

The method works well with children of all abilities and with bilingual pupils, as it offers the security of a detailed framework and a bank of appropriate vocabulary together with the challenge of a grammar and writing features component for each unit. As the grammar section contains examples from the story, all the children can access it at some level: it is not always necessary to understand the mechanics of the grammar in order to modify the examples for use in an individual story.

This is the sequence of units for Year 5. The story-type and grammatical information and activities for each unit reflect and fulfil the sentence- and text-level requirements of the NLS Framework for each term.

TERM 1

UNIT 1
Genre: animal stories
Grammar and punctuation component: standard and non-standard English (S2); commas (S6).
Writing feature: presentation of characters through dialogue, action and description (T3).

UNIT 2
Genre: sports stories
Grammar and punctuation component: connectives (S3); punctuating complex sentences (S6).
Writing feature: story beginnings (T1, T11); how characters are presented (T3).

UNIT 3
Genre: magic stories
Grammar and punctuation component: direct and reported speech (S5); setting out and punctuating dialogue (S7).
Writing feature: word play (T8); metaphors and similes (T17).

UNIT 4
Genre: playscripts
Grammar and punctuation component: verbs (S8).
Writing feature: conventions of playscripting (T18).

TERM 2

UNIT 5
Genre: traditional stories – West Indies
Grammar and punctuation component: nouns and pronouns (S10); using punctuation effectively in longer and more complex sentences (S5).
Writing feature: literal and figurative language (T10).

UNIT 6
Genre: science fiction
Grammar and punctuation component: nouns and pronouns (S4); ambiguities in sentence contractions (S7); punctuation to replace intonation, pauses or gestures (S6).
Writing feature: story endings.

UNIT 7
Genre: Irish legends
Grammar and punctuation component: types of sentences; conjunctions; punctuation of complex sentences (S5).
Writing feature: direct speech.

UNIT 8
Genre: Inuit myths
Grammar and punctuation component: constructing sentences (S8); commas in embedding clauses (S9).
Writing feature: heroes and villains (T8).

TERM 3

UNIT 9
Genre: stories from India
Grammar and punctuation component: prepositions (S3); using punctuation marks accurately in complex sentences – dashes and brackets (S4).
Writing feature: features of texts from different cultures (T1).

UNIT 10
Genre: stories in letters
Grammar and punctuation component: paragraphs; apostrophe of possession (S5).
Writing feature: narrative viewpoints (T7).

Fox Hole Inn

Fox Hole Inn stands between two settlements. Sixty years ago, people travelling from one settlement to the other stopped there for food and drink. Travellers, trappers, hunters and those seeking gold in the Great River walked along the track that ran past Fox Hole Inn. Most of them would stay for a night or so. Now, a main road had been built between the settlements and Fox Hole Inn was left behind, a tumbling, semi-derelict sprawl of a building. An old man still lived there. He sometimes came into a settlement for stores, but no one liked him. He walked with a juddering limp that made his bent and bony body sway grotesquely. He also had a nasty temper. People kept out of his way. Sometimes the braver children threw stones at him. He would growl at them like a wild animal.

Kirsty was frightened of him, but she was frightened of many things. She was frightened of her father who shouted at her. She was frightened of losing her mother, who treated her kindly and gently loved her, but looked worn out with care and work. The children in her settlement frightened her because they tormented her for being poor and small and too frightened to talk to anyone.

One day a gang of children followed her, calling her names. Kirsty began to run. She ran and ran, stumbling along the old forest track, the children throwing sticks and making howling noises. She fell over a pothole in the track and gashed her leg. The children gathered round her in a circle, chanting names. She saw someone lifting up a stick to hit her. She closed her eyes waiting for the blow to come. From nowhere the old man appeared, roaring at the children. They ran off, scattering like leaves before a gust of wind. The old man picked her up.

"I sawed what they did, the varmints. You'd better come with me and get that knee fixed," he growled. "Fox Hole Inn's just round that bend. Come on."

He grasped her hand and they limped along the track.

Inside Fox Hole Inn, Kirsty sat on an old table, a drink of milk in a dirty glass clenched in her hand. The old man sat down, rolled a cigarette and, glaring at her, drank beer from a cracked mug.

"What're you thinking?" he barked suddenly.

Startled, Kirsty blurted out exactly what she had been thinking.

"I was wondering if you've ever was loved."

He stared at her, put down his mug and said, "You're a scared little thing and that was a brave thing to say. So I'll tell you.

"Once, once I was loved. When I was your age, I had no ma and pa like you've got. I lived here with my aunt and uncle who ran this place. They didn't love me. I got leftover food to eat. I worked for them from the moment the sun rised up over those trees out there to when the last customer had dragged himself drunk to his bed. I slept outside in the shed. I knew nothing of love. The only attention I got was the beatings from my aunt and uncle.

"Then one day, a vixen and her cub were seen in the clearing that used to be in front of Fox Hole Inn, before those trees out there growed up to its door. A customer got his gun and shot the vixen. She ran, bleeding, into the forest, her cub following closely at her heels. That night, after work, I went in search of the wounded vixen, wondering what had happened to her. I found her lying dead in the forest, her cub whimpering by her side. The fox cub reminded me of myself – young, helpless and scared. The next night I saved my scraps of food and went back to where I'd found him. He had hid in the bushes near his ma's body. I waited, holding out the food. Bit by bit, the frit fox cub crawled out, his body flattened against the forest floor, his whole little frame shook with fear. But I knew that hunger makes critters do things that aren't normal – didn't I put up with everything just to survive myself? The fox cub took the food from my hand and ran back to the bushes.

"Night after night I came with food and water for that little creature. He became braver as time went on. After a while he would come right out of the bushes as I approached. He would sit next to me and eat his food and I would tell him about the hurts and cruel words that made my days. I called him Comfort. He was the only living thing I knowed that was glad to see me or would listen to a word I said.

"Soon every moment I had free I would spend with Comfort. I would use any excuse to go into the forest – collecting sticks for the fire, telling the trappers and hunters I would find animals for them – anything. Whenever I was in the forest, I would call for Comfort

and somehow he always found me and came. He began to catch his own food, small birds and rabbits. He often brought me something too. I would light a fire and cook his gift to me. Sometimes we would doze by the fire, his head in my lap.

"As I wandered round the forest doing whatever chores I was supposed to do there, he would follow me. If I stopped to climb a tree, or pick berries, he would sit, his head cocked to one side, as if he was puzzled by my strange behaviour. Comfort, who could be a darn fool, teased me too. He might wander off, then leap out at me from behind a tree, making me jump out of my skin. He would get my trouser leg between his teeth and worry it, pulling me back 'till I fell over. Then we would play fight, rolling and chasing till we threw ourselves laughing and panting on the forest floor.

"I knew happiness for the first time in my life. The beatings and hardship I knew at Fox Hole Inn never seemed so bad, because my friend was waiting for me in the forest. It was Comfort who taught me to laugh. If I was particularly sad, he always knew and would lean his head against me and lick my hand. Many a night I cried into his coat and I swear his eyes looked at me with understanding.

"One thing Comfort would never do. He would never come near Fox Hole Inn. I would get to a certain tree, five hundred yards from the edge of the clearing and he would turn and disappear into the darkness of the forest. I understood. Fox Hole Inn was a place of dread and terror to us both and there weren't nothing would induce him to come nearer."

The old man took a drag at his cigarette and sighed.

"That day we had the best time ever. It was the dead of winter. Snow lay on the ground two feet deep. There were hardly any customers and my aunt and uncle had gotten real drunk in the morning and were snoring in their beds. I decided to go off for the afternoon with Comfort and put up with the punishment I was sure to get on my return.

"Comfort and I ran and ran through the silent forest, disturbing the odd bird that rose squawking into the high blue sky. I threw snowballs at Comfort. At first he was startled; then he tried to catch them in his mouth. We tumbled together in the snow, shouting and barking with sheer joy.

"I climbed a tree to shake snow down on Comfort, who jumped and danced underneath, shaking his coat so the snow flew out like exploding jewels. I saw a nest higher up in the tree. In them days, I'm sorry to say, I had stole many a bird's egg to get us something to eat. I began to climb towards it. Comfort whined and yapped at me. I laughed down at him and told him not to be such a baby. I felt so powerful, so free, like I could fly to the treetop. Comfort started to leap up against the tree trunk, yelping, his front paws tearing at the bark. I reached up to grasp the bird's nest. My foot slipped on the branch and I was falling, falling through the black, frozen branches, the face of Comfort rushing towards me as I fell, staring at me with anguish in those tawny brown eyes.

"I thumped to the ground and a searing pain wracked through my leg. I knew it was broken. Comfort licked my face frantically, making little high sounds in his distress. I pushed him away and lifted my head. I could see a piece of bone sticking out of my leg, blood staining the snow around it. Shuddering, I lay my head down again and began to cry. Comfort pushed his head against me; he were trying to make me get up. I shouted at him to stop and he sat down suddenly, surprised because he had never heard me shout like that before. Trembling, I got up onto my elbows and pulled at the tear in my trousers above the wound, thinking I would use a strip of it as a bandage. Comfort came over and got a bit of the material between his teeth and pulled. The pain thundered through my body like an avalanche and I passed out."

The old man stopped his story. With trembling hands he rolled another cigarette and gulped down the rest of his drink. A tear rolled down his face. He wiped his nose with the back of his hand and stared down at the table. Kirsty's heart began to thud.

"What happened?" she whispered.

The old man lifted his head and looked straight at her.

"When I came to I was on a bed back at Fox Hole Inn. The grim, sneering face of my uncle stared down at me from the foot of the bed. A drunk who used to be a doctor was bandaging my leg. When he saw I was conscious he held out a flask of whisky towards me. Something at the back of my mind bothered me. I couldn't work out how I had got to Fox Hole Inn with a broken leg. 'Did I walk back?' I asked, pushing the flask away, though I badly needed the relief from pain I knew the whisky would give me.

"My uncle and the doctor laughed. Then my uncle leaned over the end of the bed, 'Don't be so stupid. If you hadn't already got a broken leg that'll give you a limp for the rest of your life, I'd give you one myself.'

"The old doctor patted my hand, 'We went out and searched for you, lad. Found you too, thank the Lord. Out cold you have been. Just as well, cos it's saved you a deal of pain from being carried back here like a sack of potatoes.' I thought for a moment. 'But how did you know what happened?' I asked. 'Shut them questions,' snapped my uncle. 'Now, now, the boy's had a shock,' wheezed the doctor. My uncle rubbed the stubble on his chin. 'Lucky for you,' he snarled, 'that we saw a fox with a bit of your trousers in its snout, though dang me if I understand what it was doing with it.'

"My heart leapt – Comfort! 'Come right up to the door it did,' my uncle continued, 'scratching at it too. I didn't never see a fox behave like that afore. Cheek of the thing, bold as brass, making scratch marks on the door an' all.' I stared at my uncle. Comfort, what was terrified of Fox Hole Inn, had torn off a piece of my trousers and had passed the tree he always stopped at five hundred yards inside the forest. Comfort had crossed the clearing where his mother had been shot. Comfort, gripping my trouser material in his teeth, had, with terror trembling in every limb, gone up to the door of Fox Hole Inn and scratched at it. Comfort had called to these people to save me. Yes, little girl, I have been loved.

"I cried out then, 'Where is he? Where's Comfort now? Please let him come in here; please bring him to me.' They stared at me. 'What are you talking about boy? Has he lost his mind?' my uncle asked the doctor. 'Now, son,' the doctor felt my head, 'quieten down and explain yourself.' I took a deep breath. 'The fox, doctor, please can you bring the fox as came, in here to me? Has he gone back to the forest?' I looked from one to the other. The doctor shook his head. 'He needs a rest. We'd better leave him.' They walked to the door. 'The fox!' I shouted. My uncle turned. 'We shot the ruddy fox. He won't bother you again.' With that my uncle left the room and my world ended. Just like that. Ended."

The room was getting dark now. Kirsty got off the table. She had to get home or she'd be in real trouble.

"I'm sorry," she murmured. "I'm so sorry. Thank you for helping me, but I'd better go now."

Kirsty took a deep breath and with more courage than she'd ever felt before said loudly, "I ain't afraid of you no more. I'll come back tomorrow with some of my ma's cakes. I … I'd like that."

But the old man wasn't listening. He was staring out of the window. Staring at the crowding forest and the black silhouettes of branches that crossed like barbed wire against Fox Hole Inn.

Understanding the grammar and punctuation

Standard English

Standard English means using English in a way we all agree to.

Non-standard English is when we write or speak in a way that is different from this.

"I _sawed_ what they did." (Non-standard English) "I _saw_ what they did." (Standard English)

"I _didn't never see_ a fox behave like that afore." (Non-standard English. This is an example of a double negative. You don't need both _didn't_ and _never_ in the same sentence.)

"I've _never seen_ a fox behave like that before." (Standard English)

Dialect and non-standard English

People from different places and different times speak differently. English is a living language and is always changing, but if someone speaks or writes in a different way from what we have all agreed to as the standard we use here and now, they are using non-standard English.

"I _sawed_ what they did, the varmints."

'Varmint' is a dialect word, often used in the USA. It means a troublesome person or animal.

Commas

Commas are used to separate items in a list. They are also used:

1 After the first phrase in a sentence: "_Sixty years ago, people travelling from one settlement to the other stopped there for food and drink._"

2 To mark off parts of a sentence that are not essential: "_She was frightened of losing her mother, who treated her kindly and gently loved her, but looked worn out with care and work._"

3 When two adjectives are placed in front of the noun they are describing: "_the black, frozen branches._"

Using standard English

Read these sentences. Decide why they are non-standard English.
Rewrite each one in standard English.

1   *I is climbing the tree.*

   _____

2   *You am coming with me.*

   _____

3   *We has fun together.*

   _____

4   *They shoots the fox.*

   _____

In the box below are some verbs that end in 'ed' when used in the past tense.

> stop   walk   live   like   frighten   shout   love   look   torment   follow

Use the verbs in the following sentences with the standard English ending.

1.   *Many travellers_____ at Fox Hole Inn.*

2.   *The old man _____ along the track.*

3.   *Kirsty _____ in a settlement.*

4.   *None of the children _____ Kirsty.*

5.   *Being chased _____ Kirsty.*

6.   *The old man_____ at the children when he saw what they were doing.*

7.   *The fox cub _____ the boy who fed him.*

8.   *The boy_____ for the fox cub in the forest.*

9.   *The boy's aunt and uncle _____ him with kicks and blows.*

10. *Comfort_____ the boy everywhere, except to Fox Hole Inn.*

On the back of this sheet, write what you think these dialect words might mean.

> varmints   afore   critters   plimsolls   happen I will   tha' knows   I ken

Commas

Read the sentences below. Decide if they need commas or not.
Add the commas where necessary.

1. The old man who had a limp lived in Fox Hole Inn.
2. The old man lived in Fox Hole Inn.
3. The little girl who was frightened was called Kirsty.
4. Kirsty was a frightened little girl.
5. The dirty glass had milk in it.
6. The glass which was dirty had milk in it.
7. The vixen and her cub ran into the forest.
8. The vixen who was wounded ran into the forest with her cub.
9. The customers all of them drunk fell asleep.
10. The drunken customers fell asleep.

Match these sentence parts. Rewrite them, using commas.

Kirsty was frightened of him	Kirsty sat on an old table.
They ran off	bleeding into the forest.
Inside Fox Hole Inn	but she was frightened of many things.
She ran	scattering like leaves.
That night	the frit fox cub crawled out.
I waited	after work I went in search of the wounded vixen.
Bit by bit	holding out the food.

_____

_____

_____

_____

_____

_____

On the back of this sheet, write four sentences of your own using commas.

Helpful hints for writing an animal story

✦ Animal stories can be about animals sharing experiences with each other or animals and humans sharing experiences with each other.

✦ Invent some interesting characters. Try to build up a picture of them inside your head – think about what they look like, how they move and how they speak and behave. Remember that, all the way through the story, the characters should move, speak and act in ways that belong to them.

✦ Animal stories often involve a search for something. The characters in your story could be searching for food, shelter, safety, freedom from cruelty, love, understanding, companionship or all of these!

✦ If you have animal characters relating to other animals or humans, write about what happens between the main characters. How do they get on? What do they do together? How do they feel about each other? When they talk, try to get your characters to talk to each other in ways that show how they feel.

✦ During the story your main characters should learn something about themselves or develop in some way. Perhaps in the beginning they are shy, but through the events of the story they have learned how to overcome this shyness. Give your characters something in the beginning of the story that will change because of what happens in the story.

✦ Most animal stories will tell us something about ourselves as humans. They will show what humans do to the natural habitats and environments of animals or they will tell us something about how some humans treat animals.

✦ Happy endings are lovely, but do not be afraid to write about sad events if you wish. The ending should, however, give a clue that something is going to be better in the future.

Animal story
Scaffold 1

You are going to write an animal story.
To help plan your story, use the framework below.
Choose one option from each stage.

Stage One

Introduce the characters and set the scene.

a) Once there were two dolphins that often swam in a small seaside bay.

b) Once there was a dolphin that often swam in a small seaside bay and who one day met a child there.

c) Once there were two dolphins that often swam in a small seaside bay and who one day met a child there.

Stage Two

Give the characters a plan / a change / an adventure.

The dolphin(s) grew to love people too much. It/they:

a) swam and played with them all the time;

b) stayed in the bay to be near the child or other people;

c) gave people rides on their backs.

Stage Three

Start the characters off on their adventure.

The dolphin(s) made a lot of money for local people because:

a) film crews came and stayed to film them;

b) crowds of people stayed in the local area to see them;

c) It/they appeared on television and in newspapers. It/they became famous. The local people made dolphin souvenirs and sold them to passing tourists.

Stage Four

Give the characters a problem.

The local people wanted to make sure the dolphin(s) stayed in the bay. They put a net across the bay. This meant that:

a) fish could not get into the bay and the dolphin(s) might starve;

b) the dolphin(s) became very unhappy at being trapped and this made it/them very ill;

c) the dolphin(s) became seriously injured from bashing against the net in an attempt to escape.

Stage Five

The problem is solved.

a) Someone who used to train dolphins, trained the dolphin(s) to leap across the net.

b) A deep-sea diver cut a hole in the net.

c) There was a public outcry about the cruelty of the net and the local people were forced to remove it.

Stage Six

Conclude the story.

a) The dolphin(s) escaped and was/were never seen again.

b) The dolphin(s) escaped and sometimes gave a show for tourists out on boat trips.

c) It was too late and the dolphin(s) died. The local people were very upset but they learned a lesson about caring for wild animals.

Animal story
Vocabulary bank 1

affection
calm
camera
close mesh net
coast
cruelty
diver
diving
dolphin
dorsal fin
drift
entertainment
escape
famous
flipper

gash, tear, rip, wound
injured
intelligent
make a break for it
mammal
marine
natural harbour
perform
playmate
public
seaside
shoreline
sicken, weaken
souvenir
splutter

starve
surface
tide
tourist
trapped
unhappy
welcome

My own words

Animal story
Scaffold 2

You are going to write an animal story.
To help plan your story, use the framework below.
Choose one option from each stage, or use your own ideas.

Stage One

Introduce the characters and set the scene.

In Africa there was:
a) a wild baby rhinoceros, a child and a hunter;
b) a wild baby leopard, a child and a hunter;
c) a wild baby elephant, a child and a hunter.

Stage Two

Give the characters a plan/a change/an adventure.

The hunter killed the baby animal's mother and brought the baby animal back to a compound in his village to be reared. The child was given the job of rearing it because:

a) the hunter was the child's father. The hunter was very strict and thought the child should have a job;
b) the hunter was the chief of the village. Rearing the animals was a very important job and the chief wanted to reward the child for something the he/she had done;
c) the child was very lonely and the only one in the community who cared for animals.

Stage Three

Start the characters off on their adventure.

The animal and the child had many shared experiences and grew to love each other.

a) This made the child more confident and able to develop better relationships with people.
b) This made the child increasingly isolated from other people.
c) When the child becomes an adult, he/she will be expected to be a hunter. The shared experiences with the animal made the child evaluate the role of the hunter and his/her own future.

WHICH ADVENTURE SHALL I CHOOSE?

Stage Four

Give the characters a problem.

The hunter decided the animal was now large enough to kill for:

a) its horn;
b) its coat;
c) its tusks.

The child was very upset about this.

Stage Five

The problem is solved.

The night before the animal was to be killed, the child opened the gate to the compound.

a) All the animals escaped and the call of the wild overcame the animal's love for the child and it, too, escaped.

b) The animal refused to go, so the child had to be brutal to the animal to make it go.

c) The child led the animal out into the wild until it was lost and then left it.

Stage Six

Conclude the story.

The hunter was furious when he discovered what the child had done.

a) The child realised that, like the animal, it was time to move on and make a new life somewhere else.

b) The uproar caused by the child's action drew attention to the hunting. The villagers learned that it was illegal to hunt animals for their horns/coats/tusks. There was a ban on hunting and the local area became a wildlife sanctuary, with the child growing up to be in charge of it.

c) The child often saw the wild animal in the surrounding area. The animal returned the child's favour of saving its life by saving the child's life in some way.

Animal story
Vocabulary bank 2

abandon
adult
anguish
animal
caring
chief
community
compound
confident
conservation
defenceless
devotion
elephant
escape
experience
ferocious
furious
future

game reserve
game warden
harsh
hunter
illegal
important
isolated
ivory
leopard
national park
on the
    scent / track / trail
pitiful
prohibit
pursue
quarry
ranger
rear

refuse
rescue
reservation
rhinoceros
ruthless
safari
sanctuary
savage
scrubland
stampede
surrounding
tough
upset
village
villagers
wilderness

My own words

Teamwork

"So, the charity fund-raising event this year," boomed the voice of the head teacher, Mrs Grant, "will be a football match between the Year 6 and Year 5 teams."

There was a cheer from the back of the hall as the Year 5 boys heard those words. Usually, the charity event was for Year 6 only. Ben Shearer and Alex Fraser beamed at each other. They both knew that Year 5 had by far the better team and the better chance of winning since Ben was the best goalie in the school and Alex had a strong reputation for his scoring abilities. Besides, Year 6 had lost most of their matches against other schools this season.

Ben and Alex felt an air of certainty about the impending match as they discussed it on their walk home after school.

"Fancy a practice before tea?" Ben suggested.

"Good idea," agreed Alex as the two boys ran excitedly up their neighbouring paths, dropping schoolbags, muddy PE kits and football boots in hallways, each making their way towards kitchen snacks.

"That sounds like a great idea," Mrs Fraser encouraged. "Will parents be invited?"

"Think so," muttered Alex, his mouth full of fruit cake. "Mrs Grant says we're getting proper tickets printed and everything."

Ben and Alex had grown up together. Since they were babies, they had been next-door neighbours: sharing toys; going to the park and playgroup together; starting school together; and, more recently, joining the local junior football team together. Ben was a natural in goal and was coached and encouraged by his father. Alex followed in his older brother's footsteps; he was a striker for a league team. Thanks to the two boys, the Cholsey Junior Football Team had won an enviable collection of trophies and shields.

The date for the charity match was announced in the next school assembly. It would be the Saturday before half-term week, which gave teams, coaches, staff and the PTA just three weeks to organise and prepare. Letters were given out

requesting help in selling tickets, refreshments, advertising, alerting local papers … the whole school would be involved in various ways. As the days passed and the training sessions became more intense, so the excitement grew and grew.

"What d'you think the score's going to be?" Alex asked Ben during the journey home after a long and wearying training session.

"Mmm, three–nil to us," grinned Ben.

Alex gaped. "Only three?"

Ben nudged him. "Kidding!"

"More like ten–nil," shouted Alex, dodging Ben's schoolbag, "and that's only if **you** don't let any in!"

The two boys shouted and cajoled each other until they reached home, exhausted.

"Never underestimate the opposition," Mr Shearer told Ben seriously as they sat down to eat that evening. "From what I've heard, Mr Cole is giving Year 6 some extra coaching, so you might have to be on your toes!"

Ben told Alex what his father had said as they sat by the goalpost after their evening practice.

"D'you think Mr Cole wants Year 6 to win?" asked Ben. "He's supposed to be **our** class teacher!"

"Nah!" replied Alex, having pondered the question for a moment. "They need all the help they can get. That Max can't score for toffee!!"

"What if we lose…?" Ben began, then stopped as he realised Alex was up and about to take a penalty kick. Ben took up his position, leapt into the air and caught the ball Alex had swiftly booted towards the goalmouth.

"See?" said Alex. "Nothing to worry about."

The next few days at school were busy: posters were designed to go in shop windows around the town; banners were made to cheer on the Year 5 and Year 6 teams; coloured streamers were created and everyone took home books of tickets to sell to family, friends and neighbours. No one in town could escape Cholsey Primary School's charity event this year.

The last training session was on Friday afternoon and suddenly, for some reason, Alex began to feel butterflies in his stomach. Nerves were not something Alex usually suffered from before a match, but today was different. Something wasn't going right. Out on the pitch, he practised his tackles, his passes and his ball-control. Although everything went like clockwork, he had an uneasy feeling and couldn't explain why. He wouldn't mention it to Ben in case he thought he was daft.

Finally, the day of the Cholsey Charity Match arrived. At half past two the teams assembled in their classrooms, ready to change into strips donated by two local, rival sports shops. Much to Alex and Ben's delight, their strip was red, the same colour as Alex's brother's team. Year 6 would play in blue.

"Cool," said Ben, admiringly as Alex adjusted his collar and ran just a tiny amount of gel through his hair. Just then, Mr Cole arrived at the classroom door, looking a little ruffled.

"Er…, we have a little problem."

Alex and Ben exchanged glances as Mr Cole fiddled with his watchstrap.

"Bit of a crisis, I'm afraid. Year 6 are a player short due to an unexpected injury. Max fell off his bike on his way here and it seems he's broken his leg."

Alex looked heavenwards. Max had a reputation for being accident-prone. Mr Cole continued, "Consequently, as both subs are ill with 'flu we'll need to 'borrow' one of you … any volunteers?"

The team shuffled, heads down, saying nothing.

"In that case," sighed Mr Cole, "we'll have to draw out a number at random."

The room fell silent. Mr Cole quickly wrote the team's numbers on separate pieces of paper and placed them inside his baseball cap. Ben was the exception. Mr Cole offered Ben the hat and told him to pick out just one. Ben knew better than to argue with Mr Cole. The team exchanged anxious glances, muttering, "Not me," and "No way," whilst Ben fiddled nervously with the folded papers before finally pulling one out and giving it to Mr Cole.

Slowly, Mr Cole unfolded the paper and announced the player who would 'defect' to the Year 6 team for this important match.

"Sorry, Alex, luck of the draw I'm afraid," Mr Cole said as he handed Alex the blue shirt. Alex felt a rush of panic and tears began to prick his eyes but he managed to fight them back. He couldn't look his team-mates in the eye, least of all Ben, and simply allowed himself to be ushered out of the classroom towards the waiting Year 6 team.

A huge roar went up as the teams poured out onto the pitch. Mrs Grant welcomed the spectators, said a few words about the proceeds from the event, then the coin was flipped and ends were chosen. The referee blew the whistle and the game began. Alex felt as if he was in a dream. Again and again, he made controlled passes, blocked tackles and worked mechanically, but his heart wasn't in it because he was terrified of having to face Ben.

At half-time, the score was nil–nil. The game continued without Alex's usual air of self-confidence and enthusiasm. Then, with two minutes to go, Jack, captain of the Year 6 team, passed the ball to Abigail, who swiftly took it down the wing towards Alex. This couldn't be happening. What was he supposed to do if he got the ball? Ben knew all of Alex's tactics and vice versa but they'd **never** played on opposing teams before. And then a penalty was awarded to Year 6. Jack gestured to Alex to take it. Everyone knew this was Alex's strong point. Taking a deep breath, Alex focused before running towards the ball. It soared high but Ben's fingers touched it, almost deflecting it. Suddenly, the ball seemed to change direction and curved over Ben's arm and into the goal mouth. The spectators cheered. Year 6 ran over to Alex and slapped him on the back. The final whistle blew. It was over. Year 6 had won one–nil. Alex hung his head as he walked slowly back to the classroom but he needn't have worried. Ben was waiting, holding out the red shirt Alex should have worn.

"Well played, mate," he beamed.

"Fancy a practice later?" asked Alex, nervously.

"You bet," grinned his friend.

Understanding the grammar and punctuation

Connectives

Connectives are words and phrases that link clauses or sentences.
There are two kinds of connective:

conjunctions *(but, if, when, because)* and
connecting adverbs *(however, meanwhile, anyway, finally)*.

Using connectives lets us create more interesting and complex sentences, rather than using too many simple, short sentences in our writing. For example:

Again and again, he made controlled passes, blocked tackles and worked mechanically. His heart wasn't in it. He was terrified of having to face Ben.

becomes:

Again and again, he made controlled passes, blocked tackles and worked mechanically, but his heart wasn't in it because he was terrified of having to face Ben.

Punctuating complex sentences

When a sentence begins with a subordinate clause, a comma is placed directly after the opening clause to make it easier for the reader to understand the sense of the sentence.

For example:

Taking a deep breath, Alex focused before running towards the ball.

Colons and semicolons

A colon (:) is used to introduce lists, speech, an idea or an explanation in a sentence. A semi colon (;) is used to divide clauses in a sentence or to separate complicated items in a list.

For example:

The next few days at school were busy: posters were designed to go in shop windows around the town; banners were made to cheer on the Year 5 and Year 6 teams; coloured streamers were created and everyone took home books of tickets to sell to family, friends and neighbours.

Connectives

Read the sentences below. Choose connectives from the box to complete each one.

> before   but   as   suddenly   since   after
> although   because   besides   whilst

1. They both knew that Year 5 had by far the better team and the better chance of winning _____ Ben was the best goalie in the school and Alex had a strong reputation for his scoring abilities.

2. Ben and Alex felt an air of certainty about the impending match _____ they discussed it on their walk home after school.

3. _____ the team had won most of their matches this season, they still had to train hard.

4. Mr Cole wanted both teams to win _____ he knew Year 5 was the stronger team.

5. Mr Cole had to borrow a player from Year 5_____ a Year 6 player was injured.

6. Alex and Ben did not want to play against each other _____ they still wanted to be in the match.

7. The teams walked onto the pitch and _____ the crowd started to cheer.

8. _____ Abigail passed the ball to Alex he scored the winning goal.

Choose three connectives from the box to write three sentences of your own.

Commas

The sentences below have been written without commas.
Place commas correctly so that each sentence makes sense.

1. *Usually the charity event was for Year 6 only.*

2. *Besides Year 6 had lost most of their matches against*
    other schools this season.

3. *Alex and Ben gathered up their football boots socks*
    shorts football shirts and kit bags and hurried out of the door.

4. *Thanks to the two boys the Cholsey Junior Football Team had won an enviable*
    collection of trophies and shields.

Read these sentences. A colon (:) and some semi-colons (;) are missing from each one. Put
them in the correct places.

1. *Alex wanted four things for his birthday a poster of his favourite footballer a*
    Manchester United strip some new studs for his boots and a computer game.

2. *The teacher wrote the following items on the board three spoonfuls of sugar two*
    cupfuls of self-raising flour two free-range organic eggs and a large mixing bowl and
    spoon.

3. *The girls took with them two large carrier bags a folding table with a broken leg a*
    large umbrella to keep off the rain and an old money tin for the change.

Write two sentences of your own using commas, colons and semicolons.

Helpful hints for writing a sports story

✦ *Select a sport that is familiar to you so you will know what to write about it in your story.*

✦ *Describe your characters carefully, giving them particular characteristics and abilities.*

✦ *Make sure some difficulty or obstacle to success occurs during your story which your character(s) has/have to overcome.*

✦ *Include some descriptions of the sporting action taking place in order to provide interest and heighten the excitement and tension.*

✦ *Include some technical sporting terms – but not too many.*

✦ *Write in the third person ('he', 'she') or the first person (I). But remember, if you write in the first person you will be limited in terms of being able to tell the story only from one character's point of view.*

✦ *You can use names for your characters that are similar to those of well-known sports personalities.*

✦ *There should be a strong element of rivalry between opposing teams/characters, contrasted with strong teamwork between characters on the same side. This will give your story a good foundation and move the action along.*

✦ *Remember to give your story a positive or happy ending.*

Sports story
Scaffold 1

You are going to write a sports story.

To help plan your story, use the framework below.

Choose one option from each stage, or two if the stage is in sections.

Stage One

Introduce the characters and set the scene.

Section A

Once there were two swimmers, Swimmer A and Swimmer B. While Swimmer A showed a good sporting attitude, Swimmer B would do whatever was necessary to win a race. They were arch-rivals. They were ambitious and trained every day.

a) They were both teenage girls.

b) They were both teenage boys.

Section B

a) There was bitter enmity between their coaches.

b) Their parents hated one another.

Stage Two

Give the characters a plan/a change/an adventure.

The swimmers found out that they had got through the trials for a really important race.

Section A

a) The winner of this race would also win a big sponsorship deal to promote sportswear.

b) This race was the decider for a place in the Olympic squad.

Section B

Swimmer A and Swimmer B, together with their parents and coaches, arrived in the city where the race was due to take place. The race was being held in:

a) London;

b) New York;

c) another city that you know well.

Unfortunately the swimmers were staying in the same hotel!

Stage Three

Start the characters off on their adventure.

On the morning of the race, Swimmer A was warming up in his/her hotel room.

a) A bouquet of flowers was delivered to the room. The flowers had a strange perfume.

b) Swimmer A opened the door to room service. He/she was pleased that his/her coach had ordered a light breakfast for him/her.

c) A 'good luck' card was pushed under the door of Swimmer A's room. Thinking it was from a fan, the swimmer opened the card and read it.

Stage Four

Give the characters a problem.

WHICH PROBLEM SHALL I CHOOSE?

a) As Swimmer A was waiting on the starting block for the race to begin, he/she started to feel unbearably tired.

b) As Swimmer A was waiting on the starting block for the race to begin, he/she started to feel dizzy.

c) As Swimmer A was waiting on the starting block for the race to begin, he/she started to feel sick.

Stage Five

The problem is solved.

a) Swimmer A heard Swimmer B's mother/coach screaming, "It's working! It's working!"

b) Swimmer A noticed that Swimmer B was laughing.

Swimmer A understood that the flowers/food/card had contained drugs. These drugs were making Swimmer A feel tired/dizzy/sick. The flowers/food/card had been sent by Swimmer B!

Swimmer A became even more determined to win the race! He/she swam the best race of his/her life, and beat Swimmer B into second place! Remember to describe the race.

Stage Six

Conclude the story.

WHICH ENDING SHALL I CHOOSE?

a) Swimmer B apologised to Swimmer A and said that it had been his/her mother's/coach's idea to cheat.

b) Swimmer B said that he/she had paid one of the hotel staff to remove the evidence. Swimmer B said, "My plan didn't work this time, but maybe next time it will!"

c) Swimmer B's coach was arrested. Swimmer B was banned from racing for good.

Sports story
Vocabulary bank 1

ambitious

arch-rivals

black lines

bursting lungs

coaches

dive

ecstatic

failure

goggles

hotel

in despair

lane ropes

lap, round

legs like lead

Olympic

oxygen

racing

red lane markers

roar of the crowd

room service

splash

sponsorship

sportswear

squad

starting block

swimmer

swimsuit

"Take your marks"

teenagers

training

water

whistle

My own words

Sports story
Scaffold 2

You are going to write a sports story.
To help plan your story, use the framework below.
Choose one option from each stage or two if the stage is in sections.

Stage One

Introduce the characters and set the scene.

Once there was a goalkeeper who repeatedly let his team down by letting in goals. The team and their manager became very angry with him and didn't want him on the team. He played:

a) for a local football club

b) for his school team

Stage Two

Give the characters a plan/a change/an adventure.

Section A
The team was about to train for a very important match. It was:

a) the County Cup

b) the County Schools' Shield

Section B
The manager/coach told the goalkeeper that unless he stopped letting in goals he would be dropped from the team. The goalkeeper knew that he would have to train hard. He decided to:

a) do some extra training very early in the mornings

b) do some extra training every weekend

Stage Three

Start the characters off on their adventure.

The goalkeeper hated training at unsociable times. Then one day someone offered to help. It was:

a) the local milkman

b) the manager's gran

To begin with, the goalkeeper's saves were few and far between but, with help, he soon improved enormously.

Stage Four

Give the characters a problem.

The goalkeeper kept his training sessions secret and didn't want anyone to know who was helping him in case he became a laughing-stock.

The day of the match was drawing nearer and one day the trainer asked for a ticket to come and see the match. While the goalkeeper was grateful for the trainer's help he panicked and said:

a) there were no more tickets available

b) the match was on another day

The trainer knew that the goalkeeper was lying and was both upset and disappointed.

Stage Five

The problem is solved.

On the day of the match the team manager/coach told the goalkeeper that he knew about the trainer and that the trainer had a secret. The team manager/coach said:

a) the milkman was his cousin and he had been a football coach for a famous team. The team manager/coach said he had arranged for the extra training.

b) his gran had once been a goalkeeper and he had asked her to help with some training.

The goalkeeper now felt a sense of relief and pride, looking forward to the match. Remember to describe the action.

Stage Six

Conclude the story.

a) The goalkeeper didn't let any goals in. His team won the County Cup!

b) The goalkeeper didn't let any goals in. His team won the County Schools' Shield!

He gave his secret trainer due credit for his success and didn't feel embarrassed any more.

Sports story
Vocabulary bank 2

action	jubilant	practise (verb)
cross bar	leaped	relief
desperate(ly)	lunged	score/scoring
determined	manager	sessions
disappointed	miserable	stretched
expression	offside	striker
famous	opportunity	success
foul	opposition	tremendous
goal	pathetic attempt	victorious
goalkeeper	penalty	victory
grasped	pitch	whistle
grateful	practice (noun)	

My own words

The Witch of Class 5B

"Right, everyone! Quiet!" called Mrs Broome, clapping her hands briskly. "David and Megan, whatever is the matter now?"

As usual, 5B were taking longer than any other class in the school to settle for afternoon registration. As usual, David and Megan were having another of their disagreements.

"You can't even spell," David mocked, holding up the animal poster Megan had been working on in Literacy.

"Yes I can," hissed Megan, trying to snatch the poster from David's taunting grasp.

"Enough!" shouted Mrs Broome over the noise. David obligingly gave Megan back her poster and sat down.

"That hurt!" yelped Megan as David sneakily prodded her with a freshly-sharpened pencil just as Mrs Broome turned to open the register.

"That does it!" Mrs Broome exploded. "Megan, you come and sit next to Zoe. David, put the pencil down. Down!" Mrs Broome sighed, tidied the bun at the back of her head and adjusted her glasses. "That's better," she said, calmly.

Wednesday afternoons were always like this. On Wednesday afternoons, 5B had science and the current topic was the life-cycle of the frog. The class had already collected frogspawn from the school's nature garden and watched daily as the tadpoles began to grow and develop. Today, they had to work in groups, drawing the stages of development.

"I'd like you all to write a sentence underneath each picture, describing each stage of the frog's life," Mrs Broome explained, scanning the class with her razor eyes.

Megan glared at David who sneered back. "Hmmph, I wish I could turn David Jackson into a frog," Megan muttered quietly.

As quick as a flash, Mrs Broome turned around from the whiteboard and pointed her marker pen at Megan with a steel gaze. "Megan Brown, shame on you!" was all she said.

Megan looked around, puzzled and embarrassed. She hadn't said it so that anyone near her could hear, so how on earth could Mrs Broome?

Megan sucked her pen, thinking hard. The more she thought, the more she could visualise nasty, ugly David as a frog. He stuck his tongue out at her and she imagined him sitting by a pond, catching flies with his long, sticky frog tongue.

At home, Megan daydreamed about turning David into a frog. She was still thinking about it as she fed Oscar.

"Only witches can turn people into frogs," Megan complained, stroking Oscar's soft, coal-black fur as he ate and purred simultaneously, "and witches have familiars. Did you know that, Oscar?"

"Of course," the cat replied, looking up from his bowl. He raised an eyebrow.

Megan, who was heading for the kitchen door, stopped in her tracks. She spun around like lightning.

"Oscar … you can speak!"

The cat sighed, "Naturally. I am your familiar and you … are a witch."

Megan gasped and asked Oscar how she could possibly be a witch.

"Humans!" tutted Oscar. "All the females in your family are witches, my dear. Now … who is it you want to turn into a frog?"

Oscar listened patiently as Megan told him all about David Jackson and his mean ways. The cat twitched his whiskers.

"Very well. I'll help," he said, "but you must remember that magic is a serious business, not to be entered into lightly. Are you sure you're up to it?"

Megan thought for a moment.

"Definitely," she nodded. "I want to get back at that David Jackson!"

"In that case," the cat considered, "we will need a spell."

It took until bedtime, but at last they had devised a spell just right for turning a boy into a frog.

At school the next morning, Megan breezed into the classroom and took her place next to David. He scowled at her, ready to snatch her pencil case and empty the contents onto the table, a ritual he performed every morning. Megan didn't flinch. She remained as cool as a cucumber, retrieving the scattered items and replacing them neatly in her pink, fluffy pencil case. David was puzzled. Normally, she retaliated with teeth and nails and hair flying, but not today. He wondered why.

After assembly, Mrs Broome began the Literacy session.

"This morning, I'd like you to write a poem," she explained, "about an animal of your choice, describing it without actually naming it."

The girls immediately went into raptures about their pet hamsters, rabbits, dogs and ponies. The boys asked if they could write about unusual pets like snakes and spiders.

"Why can't we do a poem about football or something?" David whined.

"David," Mrs Broome retorted sharply, "we have read 'Animal Poems' together in class. Were you too busy being a nuisance to listen?"

David turned red as the rest of his table sniggered.

Megan had already decided on her animal and completed her poem, decorated a border around it and handed it to Mrs Broome before anyone else. Now, she had nothing to do.

"Mrs Broome, could I please go to the nature garden?" she asked, tentatively.

Mrs Broome looked at her over the top of her glasses and nodded without saying anything.

At break, Mrs Broome gave Megan a sticker for her poem and smiled before heading off to the staff room for her coffee. Megan quickly snatched up her poem and ran outside. David was walking towards the nature garden with a large stick in his hand, no doubt intent on doing some damage. There wasn't a moment to lose.

"Oh no you don't, David Jackson, " Megan whispered, crouching behind a bush. She opened her book and began to read:

> Cold, slimy skin,
> Boggly-eyed and dim,
> Hopping from stone to stone.
> Long sticky tongue
> Jump in this pond
> And leave us all alone.

Megan looked up. David was nowhere to be seen. In his place was a large, fat frog with green, leathery skin, looking rather bewildered. It had worked.

"There," said Megan to the frog, "and you said I couldn't spell!"

"Very good, Megan." The voice behind her startled Megan and she turned as white as a sheet when she saw Mrs Broome standing there. "However, I think we should turn David back into his boy shape. I'm sure he'll turn over a new leaf now."

"But … " Megan began.

"Leave it to me," Mrs Broome said briskly. She muttered some strange words and a few seconds later, David was standing where the frog had been, looking shaken but none the worse for his adventure. Mrs Broome pointed her marker pen at him and stared at him intently. "David Jackson, you will never misbehave in class again."

David nodded sheepishly and ran off to the playground. Megan couldn't believe what she had seen.

"Mrs Broome, you're a …"

"…witch. Yes that's right," Mrs Broome said, "but don't let anyone know, will you?"

Megan shook her head, speechless.

"There's just one more thing, Megan," Mrs Broome said, sternly. "We really only have room for one witch in 5B, so no more magic in school. Agreed?" Her expression softened.

"Agreed,"nodded Megan, feeling very relieved.

Oscar, who had been watching from the fence, turned to go home.

"Humans!" he tutted in despair.

Understanding the grammar and punctuation

Direct speech

'Direct speech' refers to the words actually spoken by a character in a story.

"Right, everyone! Quiet!" called Mrs Broome.

Reported speech

'Reported speech' is where the author reports what was said by a character in a story.

Megan gasped and asked Oscar how she could possibly be a witch.

Setting out speech (dialogue)

Dialogue can be set out in four different ways:

Dialogue at the beginning of the sentence.
"You can't even spell," David mocked.

Dialogue at the end of the sentence.
The cat sighed, "Naturally. I am your familiar and you ... are a witch."

A single sentence of dialogue with narrative in between.
"In that case," the cat considered, "we will need a spell."

Two or more sentences with narrative in between.
"That does it!" Mrs Broome exploded. "Megan, you come and sit next to Zoe. David, put the pencil down. Down!"

Direct and reported speech

Look at the sentences below. Each is written in direct speech. Rewrite
each sentence in reported speech, remembering that you may have to
change the order of words or delete some words to make sense. One
has been done for you.

1. *"Very well. I'll help," he said.*

   <u>He said he would help.</u>

2. *"That's better," she said, calmly.*

   _____

3. *"I wish I could turn David Jackson into a frog," Megan muttered.*

   _____

4. *"Leave it to me," Mrs Broome said briskly.*

   _____

5. *"This morning, I'd like you to write a poem," she explained, "about an animal of*
   your choice, describing it without actually naming it."

   _____

   _____

The following sentences are written in reported speech. Rewrite each one in direct speech,
remembering to enclose the spoken words in speech marks. One has been done for you.

1. *Mrs Broome told the class to be quiet.*

   <u>"Be quiet!" Mrs Broome said.</u>

2. *Megan yelled that it hurt when David prodded her with a pencil.*

   _____

3. *Megan wished that she could turn David into a frog.*

   _____

4. *Megan gasped and asked Oscar how she could possibly be a witch.*

   _____

5. *Megan complained that only witches could turn people into frogs.*

   _____

Punctuating dialogue

Put speech marks in the correct places in the sentences below.
Use commas, exclamation marks or question marks to separate
the speech from the narrative.

1. There said Megan to the frog and you said I couldn't spell.

2. The frog looked at Megan. Croak, croak it said.

3. Don't think I'm going to take pity on you, David replied Megan fiercely.

4. And what have you been up to asked Mrs Broome who suddenly appeared.

5. Oh, uh, Mrs Broome, you surprised me responded Megan.

6. You must learn to use your magic wisely, Megan said Mrs Broome. I know it's new
    to you but you must not use it in anger.

7. But how can I turn him back into a boy again asked Megan.

8. You'd better leave that to me replied Mrs Broome as she began to make some
    loud chanting noises.

9. Hocus, pocus, thimble and bat, turn this frog into a boy again, take that yelled
    Mrs Broome.

10. David was standing there again. What on earth happened he asked.

Write some interesting dialogue to complete this paragraph. Remember to use speech marks,
commas, exclamation marks, questions marks and full stops.

Joanna raced out of the door and crashed straight into Paul as he was coming in.

_____

"Oh, sorry Paul. I'm just so excited. I need to get over to Jenny's house straight away,"
replied Joanna hurriedly.

_____

"Haven't you heard? Her cat's just had five kittens and I can't wait to see them."

_____

"Suit yourself. But I'm off. Bye," answered Joanna.

_____

Helpful hints for writing a magic story

✦ You will find it easier to tell your story in the third person, rather than the first person. This is because first person narrators can only tell the story from their own point of view. A third person narrator can tell the story from an objective point of view. For example, a third person narrator might describe how each character feels about a particular situation. A first person narrator, on the other hand, would be limited to describing their own feelings.

✦ Make your characters believable, ordinary people who have extraordinary powers or abilities.

✦ There should be at least one character who is villainous or wicked and who gets his/her just rewards.

✦ Most magic stories contain a witch/wizard and some strange magical beings such as elves or goblins. They may use traditional broomsticks, spell-books and potions or modern equivalents, such as computers and mobile phones to make their magic.

✦ Animals, who can often talk, such as cats, bats, frogs and owls, can help your hero/heroine.

✦ Use similes and metaphors to bring out the atmosphere of your story.

As quick as a flash, Mrs Broome turned around from the whiteboard.

She remained as cool as a cucumber.

✦ Use puns to create humorous or ironic effects. A pun is a play on words that sound the same but have different meanings. For example:

rose = a flower/got up

✦ Use a mixture of dialogue and reported speech for variety and to bring out aspects of your characters and their situation.

✦ Try to vary using direct speech to open a paragraph with narrative as an opening. This makes it more interesting for the reader.

✦ Give your main character some kind of task or problem to overcome in the story, using magical powers. Use your imagination in creating your setting. This could be something ordinary and everyday, such as a school or supermarket, or something strange, such as an enchanted wood or a very old building.

Magic story
Scaffold 1

You are going to write a magic story.
To help plan your story, use the framework below.
Choose one option from each stage, or more if the stage is in sections.

Stage One

Introduce the character and start the story.

Section A

a) Once there was a child. The child was the seventh son of a seventh son/seventh daughter of a seventh daughter.

b) Once there was a child who had a star-shaped mark on his/her forehead.

c) Once there was a child who had been found abandoned under a rowan tree as a baby.

Section B

a) On the child's tenth birthday, he/she received a strange letter. It was the offer of a place at a school of magic!

b) The child won first prize in a competition at Hallowe'en. The first prize was an offer of a place at a school of magic!

c) The school of magic stood on a hill at the edge of the town. The child had always wanted to be a pupil there, and on his/her tenth birthday his/her parents agreed.

Stage Two

Set the scene for an adventure.

Section A
The school was a boarding-school.

a) The school was on an island that appeared on no map.

b) The school stood on the edge of a town behind enormous wrought iron gates.

It had a potion laboratory; a broomstick gym; 100 classrooms and a spell library.

Section B
a) The head teacher was an ancient wizard.

b) The head teacher was a white witch.

Section C
a) The child made friends with a boy/girl who was brilliant at making spells.

b) The child made friends with a boy/girl who was top of broomstick-riding class.

Stage Three

Start the characters off on their adventure.

One day the friends were exploring. They sneaked into the:

a) potion laboratory;

b) library;

c) head teacher's study.

They found an ancient chest. On the lid were the words 'Do not open under any circumstances!'

They opened the chest!

Stage Four

Give the characters a problem.

a) Thousands of tiny gremlins burst out of the box! They flew round the school wreaking havoc!

b) The box was a weather box, containing mini storms, gales and hurricanes. These escaped from the room and started drenching everybody in the school!

Stage Five

The problem is solved.

a) The head teacher appeared from nowhere and made a time spell. He/she managed to turn the clock back to one hour before the friends had opened the box.

b) The head teacher appeared from nowhere and took out a wand from a case marked 'For use only in emergency'. The head teacher waved the wand and the gremlins/weather went back into the chest.

Stage Six

Conclude the story.

a) The friends had to tidy up the broomstick cupboard as a punishment.

b) The friends had to clean out the head teacher's pet dragons.

Magic story
Vocabulary bank 1

abandoned
ancient
appear
baby
birthday
brilliant
broomstick
chest
competition
cupboard
drench
emergency
enormous
escaped
exploring

flew
forehead
friend
gremlins
Hallowe'en
havoc
head teacher
island
laboratory
library
magical
nowhere
potion
riding
school

sneaked
special
spell
wand
weather
witch
wizard

My own words

Magic story
Scaffold 2

You are going to write a magic story.
To help plan your story, use the framework below.
Choose one option from each stage.

Stage One

Introduce the characters and set the scene.

Once there lived:

a) a young boy and his sister. They lived with their parents in a very old house near an ancient wood. They were extremely poor. One day their parents decided to send them to their grandparents to live at the far side of the wood;

b) two sisters whose parents had died. They lived with their aunty who was strict and cruel. Their aunty never bought them anything new and they were always hungry. One day they decided to run away;

c) two brothers who lived with their father on a run-down farm. They were very poor and never had any toys to play with. One day their father asked them to take a pig to market to sell.

Stage Two

Give the characters a plan/a change/an adventure.

As the children walked through the wood/field/park they met:

a) a strange old lady with long black hair, carrying a golden box. She asked the children to look after her box for her while she visited a friend. She warned them not to open the box no matter what happened because it was a magic box;

b) a tiny, shrivelled up man with a long nose. He was stuck fast in a hole. He asked the children to help him out and gave them a magic wand in return for their help. He told them to only use the wand if they were in trouble or danger;

c) a young boy carrying a colourful woollen rug to market. He told them that he was fed up with carrying it so he offered to give it to them in return for their shoes. The children gladly gave their shoes away because the boy told them it was a magic carpet, but he warned them not to ever sit on it.

Stage Three

Start the characters off on their adventure.

The children decided to open the box/wave the wand/sit on the carpet. The following magical thing happened:

a) A huge puff of smoke appeared and some magic dust fell onto each child. The children were covered in tiny sparkling stars.
b) A loud roaring noise was heard and the children began to spin around really fast.
c) A strange mist appeared that enveloped the children.

Stage Four

Give the characters a problem.

a) The children turned into mice and began scurrying around the wood/field/park. They were very worried about what would happen to them next. Suddenly a hungry cat appeared.
b) The children found that they were flying! They were having a great time until they realised that they didn't know how to stop!
c) They discovered that if they pointed at something it would start dancing and never stop. This was great fun until they pointed at each other! They soon became exhausted and couldn't stop.

Stage Five

The problem is solved.

a) The old lady/man/young boy reappeared, said some magic words and the children returned to normal. The old lady/man/young boy was very cross that they had wasted the magic.
b) A wizard appeared before them. He told them that he would help them only if they promised never to use the box/wand/carpet again.
c) Suddenly the children could feel themselves falling asleep. When they awoke they were in the house of the old lady/man/young boy.

Stage Six

Conclude the story.

a) The old lady/man/young boy/wizard decided to teach the children how to do magic properly. Thereafter they used their magic for only good things.
b) The children decided never to meddle with magic again. They continued on their way determined to always do what they were told from then on.

Magic story
Vocabulary bank 2

amazing

ancient

angry

appeared

bravely

colourful

continued

cruel

determined

discovered

enveloped

exhausted

extremely

flew

flying

frightened

golden

grandparents

hungry

magical

market

meddle

promised

properly

reappeared

relieved

roaring

scary

scurrying

shrivelled

sparkling

spinning

swirling

trouble

wand

warned

wasted

wizard

woollen

worried

My own words

Dinner with the Giants

CAST

NARRATOR	An Owl
GARTH	A Giant
HULK	A Giant
PAUNCH	A Giant
DIPPER	A Thief
SIMEON	A Sprite who can change shape

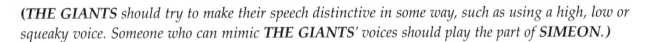

Plus non-speaking parts for **THREE ELVES**

*(**THE GIANTS** should try to make their speech distinctive in some way, such as using a high, low or squeaky voice. Someone who can mimic **THE GIANTS'** voices should play the part of **SIMEON**.)*

ACT 1
SCENE 1

*(It is night time. **THREE GIANTS** are sitting round a fire in the mountains, noisily roasting chickens. **DIPPER** is hiding behind a rock watching them. **THE OWL** is perched far stage left.)*

OWL: It is always a bad thing to be near hungry mountain giants at night. How Dipper came to be in this situation was told to me by my friend, The Shape-Changer Sprite, Simeon.

A naughty witch had cast a spell on the elves. This spell made them hiccup all the time. Simeon and the elves asked a well-known thief, Dipper, to go with them to see if he could steal a spell to stop the hiccups. They had heard that such spells could be stolen from a town full of witches that lay over the mountain. On their journey, they had stopped for the night at the foot of the mountain. Simeon had gone off to find some water and the three elves had sent Dipper to investigate a light they could see further up the mountain. Dipper had climbed silently up until he came across the giants. He was hiding behind a rock, watching the giants eating their supper. He was frightened that the giants might catch him.

*(There is a sudden crash as one of **THE GIANTS** throws a chicken onto the fire.)*

GARTH:	Chicken, rabbits, frogs! Always blinkin' animals.
HULK:	Feels like I was a nipper since the last time I had eaten humans. What we doin' 'ere anyways I don't know. And now the flippin' booze is running out.

(*HULK jogs PAUNCH's elbow just as PAUNCH is about to take a gulp of his drink. PAUNCH chokes.*)

PAUNCH:	'Ere you lot. Stop yer moaning. Do yer expect humans ought to wander by in case you fancy a nibble of their ears? Was a time when you had been crying for a tasty bit of chicken like this.

(*PAUNCH takes a huge bite from a whole chicken. THE GIANTS are grumbling and mumbling while they eat. DIPPER moves from rock to rock and then begins to creep towards PAUNCH.*)

ACT 2
SCENE 1

OWL:	As Simeon related to me, what the little thief did next was not as stupid as it may seem. Apparently, Dipper wanted to practise the stealing technique – and stealing from a giant's bag seemed like it would be a good idea at the time.

(*DIPPER puts his hand into PAUNCH's huge bag. He pulls out an enormous watch. Immediately there is the ringing of a burglar alarm off stage. DIPPER drops the watch in amazement. PAUNCH turns, sees DIPPER and grabs him by the neck.*)

PAUNCH:	Cor lummy, Garth. Good job me watch rings out if someone tries to nick it. 'Ere, look what I've collected!
GARTH:	What the 'eck is it?
PAUNCH:	Blowed if I know. (*Addressing DIPPER*) What are you?
DIPPER:	Let me go.
HULK:	A letmego? Letmegoes have been pinchin' watches from our bags while we try and have a quiet bit o' supper then, aye?
GARTH:	I bet it tastes nice.
HULK:	(*Picking up a skewer*) Only one way we will find out.
PAUNCH:	Yuck. It's all dirty and smelly. We will be taking off its skin and finding nothing but bones underneath.

GARTH:	Might be a flock of 'em letmegoes about though. We could catch 'em and, with a bit of pastry, we shall have made ourselves a tasty letmego pie. (*Addressing* **DIPPER**) Is there a flock of you a-flapping around here, eh?
DIPPER:	Oh yes … I mean, no, no, there's only me.
HULK:	What d'yer mean?
DIPPER:	What I said. Only please don't skin me and cook me. I'd taste awful. I'll do anything you ask.
PAUNCH:	He's frightened. Set him free.
GARTH:	When he's told us what he means when he says there's a flock of letmegoes and then he says there's only him. He was a pinchin' your watch, don't forget. If there's lots of 'em, we might all get robbed and killed while we sleep. We need to start skinning him till he talks.
PAUNCH:	Oh no you don't. I caught him. He's mine and I says set him free.
HULK:	You're addled, Paunch. You're an addle brain.
PAUNCH:	And you're a dim wit.
HULK:	Dim wit am I? Take THAT!

(**HULK** *pokes* **PAUNCH** *and* **THE GIANTS** *start fighting with a lot of noise.*)

SCENE 2

(**THE GIANTS** *continue to fight. During the fighting* **DIPPER** *gets knocked to the ground and is dazed.*)

ACT 3
SCENE 1

OWL:	The giants' fighting made so much noise that the elves crept up one by one to see what was happening. However, they hiccuped so loudly as they came near, the giants stopped fighting for enough time to tie each one up before they started fighting again. They forgot about Dipper who crept behind a rock again.
	Simeon had returned to the elves' camp and found that everyone had disappeared, but he heard the noise the giants made. He changed himself into a bird and flew up to where the fight was going on. He saw three elves tied up and Dipper hiding behind a rock.

SCENE 2

HULK: Stop fighting! Let's get on with roasting these elves so's we can eat them later.

SIMEON: (*Mimicking PAUNCH's voice*) It'd take too long to roast 'em now.

GARTH: Stop arguing, Paunch. We've decided.

PAUNCH: I'm not arguing.

GARTH: Yes you are.

PAUNCH: Liar. I'm not.

(*THE THREE GIANTS start fighting again.*)

SCENE 3

(*THE THREE GIANTS finally stop fighting and lie on the floor, exhausted.*)

HULK: He's right though. It'd take all night to roast 'em.

PAUNCH: I never said.

GARTH: Did.

PAUNCH: Didn't.

HULK: Shut up. I say we chop 'em and boil 'em.

GARTH: That would cook 'em quick enough.

PAUNCH: All right, all right. Get the saucepan out and find yer choppers.

ACT 4
SCENE 1

(*THE GIANTS get out a huge saucepan and after much fussing about, find their axes and begin to sharpen them.*)

SCENE 2

SIMEON: (*Mimicking HULK's voice*) It's no good boiling 'em. We ain't got no water and it's a long way to the river.

GARTH: Shut up Hulk, or we'll never get to eat them.

PAUNCH: Yeh Hulk, and you can go and get the water for moaning.

HULK: Don't you tell me to shut up and who's a-moaning? It weren't me.

PAUNCH: You liar Hulk; you big booby.

HULK: You're the liar Paunch and booby yerself.

*(**THE THREE GIANTS** start fighting again.)*

SCENE 3

GARTH: Look, if we keep on fighting, the elves will rot before we get to eat 'em. I
              say we mash 'em and boil 'em later.

SIMEON: (*Mimicking **HULK**'s voice)* Who shall we mash first?

GARTH: Better mash the last one first.

HULK: Stop talking to yerself, Garth. Anyways, which was the last one?

GARTH: That one with the loudest hiccups.

SIMEON: (*Mimicking **PAUNCH**'s voice.)* Rubbish, the last one was the one with the
              quietest hiccups.

GARTH: I knows what I'm talking about, Paunch – the last one 'ad the loudest
              hiccups.

PAUNCH: Yes, he definitely had the loudest hiccups.

GARTH: So why did you say he had the quietest hiccups then?

PAUNCH: I never said; Hulk said it.

HULK: No I never; you did.

GARTH: Hulk and I says you said it, so shut up.

PAUNCH: Who are you tellin' to shut up?

HULK: Stop arguing – remember the saying among us mountain giants 'Never
              waste time near dawn' – let's get cookin'.

SIMEON: (*Mimicking **PAUNCH**'s voice)* Dawn come and stone you!

ACT 5
SCENE 1

*(Sunlight appears over the mountain top and just as **THE THREE GIANTS** set to fighting again, they are turned to stone by the sunlight. **SIMEON**, as himself again, moves to centre stage, bringing **DIPPER** from behind the rock with him.)*

SCENE 2

DIPPER: Simeon! That was your voice causing them to argue until sunrise turned them into stone. You've saved us all from being part of a recipe. If it weren't for you we will have been cooking in a pot.

SIMEON: Well, in case you are ever with giants again, Dipper, consider this magic rune:

*(**SIMEON** spreads his arms and lifts his head. There is complete silence.)*

> Sunrise flutter the dark wings of nights
> 'Til the gloomy heavy shades have flown,
> And icy dreams tangling fear and fights,
> Are left behind and turned to stone.

SCENE 3

*(The mountain is now lit by brilliant sunshine. **SIMEON** and **DIPPER** untie the still-hiccuping **ELVES**. There is much hugging and shaking of hands. **THE ELVES** and **DIPPER** walk anxiously and curiously around the stone **GIANTS**. **SIMEON** looks on. Then, arm in arm, **THE ELVES**, **DIPPER** and **SIMEON** exit.)*

SCENE 4

*(**OWL** stands still centre stage and spreads his wings.)*

OWL: The adventures of Simeon, Dipper and the Elves were just beginning. Will Dipper be able to steal the spell to stop the hiccuping? Will Simeon and the Elves be able to keep Dipper out of trouble until he does? Will Dipper learn his lesson and never steal again?

(The stage darkens; there is a clap of thunder and a flash of lightening. The light on stage dims until there is a blackout.)

Understanding the grammar

Verb tenses

A tense is to do with time; the past, the present or the future. One test of whether a word is a verb or not is to see if you can change the tense of the word. If you can – it's a verb!

The past tense of 'He eats the letmego,' will be one of the following.

'He ate the letmego', 'He was eating the letmego', 'He has eaten the letmego', 'He has been eating the letmego', 'He had eaten the letmego' or 'He had been eating the letmego'.

The present tense of 'He eats the letmego,' will be one of the following.

'He eats the letmego,' or 'He is eating the letmego'

The future tense of 'He eats the letmego' will be one of the following.

'He will eat the letmego', 'He will be eating the letmego', 'He will have eaten the letmego' or 'He will have been eating the letmego.'

Verb forms

In an **active** sentence the writer makes it clear who is doing the action of the verb.

'The giants ate the letmego.'

Here it is clear that the giants did the eating!

In an **interrogative** sentence, questions are asked. Sometimes these have yes/no answers.

'Are you a letmego?'

Sometimes the question begins with a 'wh' word like 'where', 'who' or 'what'. These questions want than 'yes' or 'no'.

'What are you?'

In an **imperative** sentence, the verb is used to give an order or instruction or asks you to think about or compare something.

'Stop arguing!'
'Fry the letmego with onions.'
'Don't be afraid.' 'Come quickly!'
'Consider this magic rune.'

Auxiliary verbs

These are verbs that go with the main verb of the sentence. They show what has happened, is happening or will or may happen.

'He will eat the letmego.' – 'will' is an auxiliary verb that goes with the verb 'eat'.

Verbs

Put these sentences into the past and future tenses.

1. Simeon mimics Paunch's voice.

_____

_____

2. Dipper creeps towards the giants.

_____

_____

3. The Owl is sitting on a rock.

_____

_____

Put these sentences into the present tense.

1. Dipper was stealing from Paunch's bag.

_____

2. Garth had eaten chicken.

_____

3. The group had been searching for the spell.

_____

Use the following auxiliary verbs in three sentences each, one past, one present and one future:

> _To be, to have, to do, can, could, may, might, must, will, should._

Continue on the back of this sheet.

Name

Playscripts

Set out the text below on another sheet of paper in the format of a playscript. Remember to use acts, scenes and stage directions. Put in punctuation marks such as question marks and exclamation marks and font types such as **bold** and *italics*:

The characters in the play are Mary, her dog, Ugly and Nasty. Mary is a little girl and Ugly and Nasty are giants.

In the beginning, Mary is sitting in her garden on her own. She hears a loud thumping noise and Ugly and Nasty look over her garden wall and see her.

Mary asks who they are.
Ugly says he is a hungry giant who wants to eat her.
Nasty says he wants to roast her with potatoes.
Mary is frightened and asks the giants how she can stop them from eating her.
Ugly says only by giving him something nice to eat.
Nasty says it must have potatoes with it.

Next Mary is in her kitchen looking for food. She finds a big chicken in the fridge and some potatoes.

Next Mary is in the garden giving the food to Nasty and Ugly.
They say thank you and eat the chicken and potatoes raw and go away.
Mary says to her dog that the raw chicken and potatoes will give the giants a tummy ache and that it serves them right.

Next the giants are sitting in a field rubbing their tummies and moaning.
They say they will never frighten a human again.

Helpful hints for writing a playscript

◆ List your characters at the top of the page. Use capital letters for the characters' names. Don't have too many characters (2–6 are enough).

NARRATOR	An owl
GARTH	A giant
HULK	A giant
PAUNCH	A giant
DIPPER	A thief
SIMEON	A sprite

Plus non-speaking parts.

◆ Make your script simple. Divide it into main sections or 'acts'. Then divide the acts into 'scenes'.

◆ Write the opening scene. Try to imagine what it might look like on a stage.

> Scene 1
>
> (It is night time. THREE GIANTS are sitting round a fire in the mountains, noisily roasting chickens. DIPPER is hiding behind a rock watching them. THE OWL is perched far stage left.)

◆ Next, write the dialogue. Keep it simple. Write the character's name on the left-hand side of the page, leave a space and then write what the character says. Keep what the character says in lines that start at the same place.

OWL: It is always a bad thing to be near hungry mountain giants at night. How Dipper came to be in this situation was told to me by my friend, the Shape-Changer Sprite, Simeon.

◆ Remember to include stage directions. Put these in brackets.

> (There is a sudden crash as one of THE GIANTS throws a chicken onto the fire.)

◆ Think of interesting things for your characters to do. What exciting things happen to them?

◆ Make each scene end in an exciting way so that the audience will want to know what happens next.

> (DIPPER moves from rock to rock and then begins to creep towards PAUNCH.)

◆ Make sure you have a good ending.

> (The stage darkens; there is a clap of thunder and a flash of lightening. OWL spreads his wings and stands still centre stage. The light on stage darkens until there is a blackout.)

Playscript
Scaffold 1

You are going to write a playscript.
To help plan your play, use the framework below.
Choose one option from each stage.

Stage One

Choose the characters for your play.

Choose a name for each one. List them at the top of your page.

a. Three ogres asleep on a mountain, and a child.

b. Three ogres asleep in a forest, and a child.

c. Three ogres asleep in a country park, and a child.

Stage Two

Set the scene for the play.

Use this information to write the dialogue for Act 1, Scene 1. The child's parent is very sick. To save the parent the child has to find:

a. A magic flower

b. A magic tree

c. A magic fruit.

Stage Three

Start the characters off on their adventure.

Use this information to write the dialogue for Act 1, Scene 2. The child comes to where the ogres are sleeping and finds what he or she is looking for.

a. The child shouts and laughs in delight, making a lot of noise.

b. When the child takes the magic object or a piece of it, the magic object makes a loud sound.

c. There is a sudden, loud thunderstorm.

Stage Four

Give the characters a problem.

Use this information to write the dialogue for Act 2, Scene 1.

The noise wakes up the ogres.

a. They are very cross at being woken up and want to eat the child.

b. They wake up very hungry and want to eat the child.

c. They think the child looks very tasty and they want a snack!

Stage Five

The problem is solved.

Use this information to write the dialogue for Act 2, Scene 2. The child uses a part of the magic object to:

a. Send the ogres back to sleep.

b. Make food fall down from the sky.

c. Make the child look and smell like the one thing the ogres hate to eat.

Stage Six

Conclude the play.

Use this information to write the dialogue for Act 2, Scene 3.

a. The child is very happy and finds that there are lots of magic objects in the area. The child goes home.

b. The child goes home with the magic object and cures the sick parent.

c. The child takes the magic object home with extra seeds to grow the object at home.

I MUST REMEMBER TO MAKE THE ENDING GOOD.

Playscript
Vocabulary bank 1

appetite	heal	shoot
arouse	jangle	shower
bean	leaf	slumber
blast	meadow	sprinkle
bloom	medicine	sprout
blossom	monster	stalk
bough	mouldy	starving
bruiser	pasture	steep
bud	peace	stem
bulb	peal	stretch
crest	petal	temper
crop	pod	twig
din	racket	undergrowth
disgusting	rage	weed
enchanted	ridge	yawn
fury	rough	
grove	seedling	

My own words

Playscript
Scaffold 2

You are going to write a playscript.
To help plan your play, use the framework below.
Choose one option from each stage.

Stage One

Choose the characters for your play. Give each one a name. List them at the top of your page.

a. Five children.
b. Two teachers and three children.
c. Two members of a ship's crew and three children.

They are on board a ship in a terrible storm.

Stage Two

Give the characters a plan/a change/an adventure.

This will be the dialogue for Act 1, Scene 1.
The characters:
a. swim ashore;
b. find themselves on a huge piece of wood that has broken off the ship. It floats ashore;
c. wake up from being unconscious. They have been washed ashore.

The characters are on a desert island.

Stage Three

Start the characters off on their adventure.

Use this information to write the dialogue for Act 1, Scene 2.
The characters begin to search for food and water, but they can't find any so:

a. They begin to starve and get increasingly grumpy.

b. They eat disgusting things (get the characters to describe these).

c. They find small bits of food in their pockets.

Stage Four

Give the characters a problem.

Use this information to write the dialogue for Act 1, Scene 3.

If they don't eat soon, they will die. They decide they will have to resort to cannibalism. The first person to be a meal is voted for because:

a. They are the least useful.

b. They are the least popular.

c. They will make the best meal.

Stage Five

The problem is solved.

Use this information to write the dialogue for Act 2, Scene 1. The person voted for tricks the others by:

a. Setting a trap they will fall into.

b. Changing the factor that got them voted for.

c. Using their knowledge of plants to make a drink that makes the others hallucinate in some way.

Stage Six

Conclude the play.

Use this information to write the dialogue for Act 2, Scene 2.

a. A ship appears on the horizon.

b. Food is washed ashore from the shipwreck.

c. The characters build a boat and set sail.

Playscript
Vocabulary bank 2

aching void	foul	ooze
antagonise	fury	ostracise
appetizing	gale	palatable
bait	gigantic	perish
bitter	hollow	pungent
bleak	hostile	putrid
brackish	impenetrable	rank
carnivorous	imperative	ration
coast	indolent	ravenous
crave	ineffectual	rejected
crustacean	isolated	repellent
delicious	jetsam	rotting
desolate	jungle	shiftless
drenched	lethargy	tarantula
entice	lure	tempest
flotsam	meaty	useless
forsaken	nauseate	vegetarian

My own words

Anansi and Hate-to-be-contradicted

There once was a man called Hate-to-be-contradicted, which is a strange name. He got the name because he was very bad-tempered and couldn't help disagreeing with people. One morning, a villager called on Hate-to-be-contradicted and they sat beneath his palm-tree as the sun beat down like fire. As they sat talking, some palm-nuts fell to the ground.

"Hate-to-be-contradicted," said the villager, "your palm-nuts are ripe."

"No, they're not."

"Yes, look. Some have fallen. They're ready for picking."

"They are not ripe."

The villager was puzzled by Hate-to-be-contradicted's answer. Just then, some more palm-nuts fell to the ground.

"See, more ripe palm-nuts have fallen," he exclaimed.

Hate-to-be-contradicted grew hot and angry as he realised he was being contradicted.

"My palm-nuts will be ready when I say so and not before!" he shouted at the villager. "When palm-nuts are ripe, all the bunches on a branch open at the same time with a noise like a clap of thunder and they tumble down on the head of anyone who disagrees with me. What do you think of that?"

"I think you are very stupid and very rude," said the villager, staring straight at Hate-to-be-contradicted.

"How dare you?" shouted Hate-to-be-contradicted, chasing the villager out of his courtyard with a stick in his hand. "You deserve a good beating for contradicting me!"

Over the next few months, Hate-to-be-contradicted had many disagreements and he became even more bad-tempered. He hit his neighbour with a broom because he would not agree that Hate-to-be-contradicted's dog had fewer fleas than his own. He threw his brother-in-law into a pond for refusing to agree that the moon was made of curdled cow's milk. Worst of all, he threw his cooking pot at some men for saying that the sun rose over their village before it rose over Hate-to-be-contradicted's village.

The head of the village decided to ask Anansi, the spider, for advice. Anansi agreed to go and talk to Hate-to-be-contradicted. It was spring, the time of year when, once again, the palm-nuts were ripe.

"Good morning, Hate-to-be-contradicted," Anansi greeted him. "What a fine day it is."

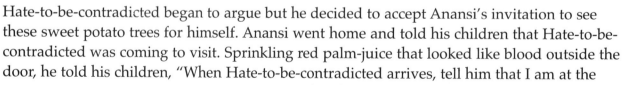

Hate-to-be-contradicted was just about to disagree when he managed to stop himself. They sat beneath the shade of a palm-tree and, as they were talking, some ripe palm-nuts fell to the ground. Hate-to-be-contradicted told Anansi his story about how to tell when palm-nuts were *really* ripe.

When he had finished, Anansi said, "I am sure that what you say is true. I have heard the thunderous sound when the bunches open at the same time, but you must come and see my sweet potato trees. They are so tall that I have to take my bow and arrow and shoot the sweet potatoes down one by one. What do you think of that, Hate-to-be-contradicted?"

Hate-to-be-contradicted began to argue but he decided to accept Anansi's invitation to see these sweet potato trees for himself. Anansi went home and told his children that Hate-to-be-contradicted was coming to visit. Sprinkling red palm-juice that looked like blood outside the door, he told his children, "When Hate-to-be-contradicted arrives, tell him that I am at the blacksmith's, having my arm mended."

Hate-to-be-contradicted was furious that Anansi was not there to greet him but he tried to control his temper.

"Where is your mother?" he asked Anansi's children.

The children enjoyed telling tales. "When she was down at the stream today, she dropped her waterpot. While it was falling, she remembered the meal she had left cooking, so she came back to take the cooking-pot off the fire. Now she has gone back to catch the waterpot."

Hate-to-be-contradicted was beside himself with rage but still, he managed to control himself. When Anansi came back, he invited Hate-to-be-contradicted to supper. The children served him a small fish on a huge pile of very hot peppers. Hate-to-be-contradicted took one mouthful and his mouth was an inferno.

"Water," he gasped.

Anansi turned to his eldest child and asked her to bring some water for their guest. A moment later, she reappeared without any water.

"I am very sorry," the child explained, "but there is no water to spare. The water at the top of the pot belongs to father. The second layer is mother's and the bottom layer is our grandmother's. So, there is no water left for you."

Hate-to-be-contradicted exploded with fury.

"You lying offspring of a spider …" he began, but Anansi stopped him with a sharp look.

"Mr Hate-to-be-contradicted," he said, "that isn't very polite. You are contradicting us. You have beaten other people for contradicting you so now we shall have to beat you!"

So, Anansi and his children beat Hate-to-be-contradicted until he broke into pieces. The pieces broke into smaller pieces and they were ground to powder which blew away on the wind to the far corners of the Earth. That is why there is a little bit of Hate-to-be-contradicted in everyone, everywhere.

Understanding the grammar and punctuation

Nouns
Nouns are words for people, places or objects.

There are two main types of noun.
Common nouns refer to ordinary objects, such as *fire* and *water*.
Proper nouns refer to names of people, places, organisations, days of the week, months and so on: *Anansi, Earth* (the planet) and *August*.

A **noun phrase** can be just one word, for example: *Anansi*; or a group of words, for example: *a huge pile of very hot peppers.*

A noun phrase can include a **determiner**, for example: **some** *palm-nuts*.

Pronouns
Pronouns are words that stand in place of nouns.

There are several types of pronoun, including:
Personal pronouns: *I, you, him, it*
Possessive pronouns: *my, your, our, his/hers*

It is important to remember that pronouns and verbs must agree:
  I am   I was
  You are   You were

When we use pronouns, it is important to make it clear to the reader who the pronoun refers to, for example:

Hate-to-be-contradicted grew hot and angry as he realised he was being contradicted.

We know that the pronoun 'he' refers to Hate-to-be-contradicted because his name has been used at the beginning of the sentence.

Complex sentences
A complex sentence contains a main clause and one or more subordinate clauses.

Commas in complex sentences
If a sentence begins with a subordinate clause, a comma is used directly after the opening clause.

A moment later, she reappeared without any water.

Nouns and pronouns

Read the following passage.
Underline the nouns and noun phrases.

There once was a man called Hate-to-be-contradicted, which is a strange name. He got the name because he was very bad-tempered and couldn't help disagreeing with people. One morning, a villager called on Hate-to-be-contradicted and they sat beneath his palm-tree as the sun beat down like fire. As they sat talking, some palm-nuts fell to the ground.

"Hate-to-be-contradicted," said the villager, "your palm-nuts are ripe."

"No, they're not."

"Yes, look. Some have fallen. They're ready for picking."

"They are not ripe."

The villager was puzzled by Hate-to-be-contradicted's answer. Just then, some more palm-nuts fell to the ground.

Complete the following sentences, choosing an appropriate pronoun from the list to fill the gaps. Remember to make the pronoun and verb agree.

> **his they I her she you**

1. "_____ are not ripe. "

2. "My palm-nuts will be ready when _____ say so and not before!"

3. "What do _____ think of that?"

4. "When _____ was down at the stream today, she dropped _____ water-pot."

5. Hate-to-be-contradicted took one mouthful and _____ mouth was an inferno.

6. Anansi turned to _____ eldest child and asked _____ to bring some water for their guest.

Complex sentences

Add commas to these sentences to make them easier to read.

1. After visiting her elderly uncle Sarah went to the supermarket to get her weekly groceries.

2. Over the next few months Hate-to-be-contradicted had many disagreements and he became even more bad-tempered.

3. Although the day was very cold Tom still went for a very long bike ride with his two friends.

4. We were running very late but we arrived just in time for my grandfather's birthday.

5. Although my friend is only ten years old she can play the piano really well.

6. After the party my mum said she knew we were up to something but she didn't let on that she knew about her surprise visitor.

Make one complex sentence by joining each pair of sentences below with a suitable connective.

1. He hit his neighbour with a broom.

   His neighbour would not agree that Hate-to-be-contradicted's dog had fewer fleas than his own.

   _____

   _____

2. Their mother looked very surprised.   The boys came home early.

   _____

3. Suddenly the lights failed.   We were left in the darkness.

   _____

4. The rioters caused some damage.   The police arrived.

   _____

Helpful hints for writing a traditional West Indian story

✦ Most traditional West Indian stories are based on legends which came to the Caribbean from Africa.

✦ Traditional stories usually have a third person narrator who sees everything omnisciently (someone who sees and knows all things).

✦ Your main characters will probably earn their living from some type of farming or working on the land. Nature is very important in West Indian stories.

✦ Anansi appears in many West Indian and West African tales. He is a trickster who sometimes looks like a man and sometimes looks like a spider.

✦ You can use a character like Anansi or an animal with human characteristics to help the other characters in your story. Usually, they provide help in the form of moral or spiritual guidance. They can, however, have some amusing and entertaining qualities.

✦ West Indian stories usually have a moral or a strange 'twist' at the end.

✦ Music is an important part of West Indian life and you could include some references to calypso, reggae or rap, if you wish.

✦ West Indian people wear colourful clothing and have a very relaxed and cheerful approach to life.

✦ You do not have to give all of your characters names. Some characters can be referred to by their title or, like Hate-to-be-contradicted, by an aspect of their personality.

Traditional West Indian story
Scaffold 1

You are going to write a West Indian story.
To help plan your story, use the framework below.
Choose one option from each stage.

Stage One

Introduce the characters.

Anansi and Tiger were friends.

Stage Two

Set the scene for the story.

Anansi was lazy. He wanted Tiger to gather in the harvest for him.

a) He told Tiger that, if he would help him, he would give him something precious in return.

b) He told Tiger that only tigers were important enough to gather a harvest.

c) He told Tiger that if he did not help him something terrible would happen to him.

Stage Three

Write the first part of the story.

Tiger worked hard in the field all day.

a) Anansi sat in the shade and slept.

b) Anansi spent the day visiting his friends.

c) Anansi sat watching Tiger from a distance, laughing at him for believing him.

Stage Four

Give the characters a problem.

At nightfall, Tiger came to see Anansi. He asked him for a share of the harvest for doing all the work. Anansi did not want to give Tiger his payment. He wanted to trick him.

a) He told Tiger to come back the next night .

b) He told Tiger to meet him in the woods at dawn.

c) He told Tiger to wait for him just outside the village at noon.

Stage Five

Write the next part of the story.

a) Anansi took Tiger to the lake. He told him that he had left a golden bowl at the bottom. He told Tiger to dive in and fetch it.

b) Anansi gave Tiger a huge sack. He told him it was full of maize.

c) Anansi took Tiger to a tall tree in the forest. He told tiger to climb up to the top of the tree where he would find a hidden sack of treasure.

Stage Six

Conclude the story.

a) Tiger dived into the lake again and again but the treasure was not there. Anansi had tricked him! The golden bowl was just the reflection of the moon in the water.

b) When Tiger got home, he proudly showed his wife the bag of maize. She told him that he was a fool and that Anansi had tricked him. It was nothing but a sack of sand!

c) When Tiger reached the top of the tree, he searched everywhere but could not find a sack. His movement caused the branch he was standing on to break. Tiger fell to the ground with a bump.

Tiger was angry. He went to look for Anansi. Anansi was hiding in the roof of his house. He may well still be there!

Traditional West Indian story
Vocabulary bank 1

angry	golden	noon
bottom	ground	payment
bowl	harvest	precious
break	hidden	reflection
dawn	hiding	share
dive	important	terrible
diving	lake	treasure
field	laughing	trick
forest	lazy	village
friends	maise	wife
gold	nightfall	worked

My own words

Traditional West Indian story
Scaffold 2

You are going to write a West Indian story.
To help plan your story, use the framework below.
Choose one option from each stage, or two if the stage is in sections.

Stage One

Introduce the characters and set the scene.

Anansi and Bush-rat were neighbours. They lived:

a. in a forest;

b. on a plantation;

c. in a small village.

Stage Two

Give the characters a plan/a change/an adventure.

One afternoon, Anansi's wife told him to go and find food for their twelve children. Anansi sulked and tried to get out of it because:

a. he was very lazy and didn't want to work that day;

b. he had just washed and didn't want to get dirty again;

c. he had other plans for the afternoon.

Stage Three

Start the characters off on their adventure.

Section A

Anansi set off reluctantly. In the distance, he heard someone groaning. When he went to investigate, he found Bush-rat in a clearing. He was groaning because:

a. he was trying to cut down a large, heavy bunch of bananas;

b. he was trying to carry a large, heavy bunch of bananas;

c. he had eaten too many bananas and had stomachache.

Continued on next sheet.

Continued from previous sheet.

Section B

Anansi offered to help Bush-rat in return for some of the bananas. Bush-rat:

a. had been tricked by Anansi before and wasn't happy about giving him any food;

b. agreed when Anansi assured him that the bananas were only for his wife and children;

c. gave Anansi thirteen bananas and no more.

Stage Four

Give the characters a problem.

When Anansi arrived home, he was very hungry. His wife roasted the bananas and gave them to the children. Anansi looked:

a. sad because he had looked forward to eating some of the bananas;

b. tired because he had worked hard helping Bush-rat;

c. angry because he expected some of the food for himself.

Stage Five

The problem is solved.

Anansi's wife and children felt sorry for him and promised him some of their food. They each:

a. gave him half of their food;

b. gave him a third of their food;

c. gave him a quarter of their food.

Stage Six

Conclude the story.

Anansi's wife said he could have more food when he had worked out what fraction of all of the food he had eaten. Anansi:

a. didn't know how many bananas there were to start with;

b. had too few spider legs to work it out;

c. was too lazy to try!

Anansi is still walking around trying to solve the problem!

Traditional West Indian story
Vocabulary bank 2

afternoon
agreed
Anansi
angry
anjisa (a special cloth
    worn around the
    head)
bananas
bush-rat
cheat
cunning
distance
forest
fraction

groaning
half
heavy
hungry
investigate
lazy
neighbours
plantation
problem
promised
quarter
reluctant
roasted
solve

sorry
spider
stomachache
sulked
third
thirteen
trickster
twelve
village
wife

My own words

A World of Difference

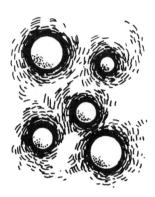

At dusk the silver orbs gathered and hung in the sky, like a still, silent flock of birds. People would remark on their shining beauty as the clouds, streaked with the colours of sunset, were reflected in their glittering shapes.

When they had first appeared everyone had panicked. Newspapers carried headlines like 'Invasion of Silver Spheres' and 'Decorations or Devastation?' Countries tried everything possible to catch or destroy them. The silver orbs, the size of tennis balls, simply zipped out of the way and carried on floating. The orbs never did any harm, but just seemed to spiral about wherever there were people. Bit by bit interest faded. They were as normal as the clouds themselves and just as elusive.

It was definitely odd, therefore, to see one bumping along the grass heading for the woods. Sarah and Jack had been arguing as usual. This time they had argued about: meteorites, black holes and eternity. Sarah was small, with a freckled, determined face and Jack was tall, dark and a bit moody. The strange sight of the silver orb rolling past them caused a moment's truce.

"I've never seen one do that before," Jack murmured.

"We'd better follow it – see what happens," Sarah said eagerly, moving forwards.

Jack caught hold of her sleeve. "Don't be silly, Sarah. It's going into the woods, it could be dangerous."

Sarah shrugged him off. "No one said you had to come if you're too scared," she snarled.

"I can't let you go on your own; something might happen to you." Jack was trying to be reasonable.

"Well, you'd better come then," Sarah said impatiently and ran off after the orb.

"You're impossible, Sarah – Sarah – wait!" Jack shouted, but she'd gone. Jack had no choice but to follow her.

The children pursued the orb as it bounced and rolled over the roots of trees, spinning deeper into the woods. There was no hope of catching it, but the orb seemed to know exactly where it was going. When it stopped, Jack and Sarah crept behind a tree, wondering what it was going to

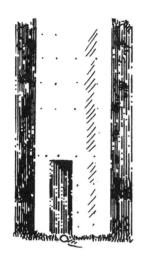

do next. As they watched, a light started to glow in front of them. It brightened and hardened into a metal cylinder as high as the trees. A gap in its side began to widen. The small silver orb rolled towards it.

"Come on Jack; it's going in. Let's follow it," Sarah whispered.

"Are you mad?" Jack screeched.

"Shush, there's no time to argue now. Coming or not? I'm going in."

Sarah darted forward again. Jack groaned, fear clutching at his stomach as he went after her. The little orb bounced through the doorway in the side of the huge metal cylinder. Sarah, followed closely by Jack, slipped in behind it: a heavy door silently slid shut behind them.

"Now look what's happened," Jack growled. "We're trapped."

The children were standing in a small, dim chamber. Low, ultraviolet light oscillated through tubes that stretched along the sheer chrome walls.

"Jack," Sarah clutched his arm, "we're floating off the ground!"

Jack looked down. His feet were hovering about five centimetres from the floor.

"It must be a slightly different gravitational pull in here," Jack said, "and we're not wearing g-suits."

Sarah wasn't too sure what g-suits were (though she wasn't going to admit that to Jack).

"So what? We can breathe. Where would we get these suits from anyway? Marks and Spencer?"

Sarah laughed and slapped her hand against the metallic wall. The sound echoed through the chamber so loudly that Sarah stopped suddenly. In the cold silence that followed, a low beeping sound began. This was followed by a mechanised voice saying, "Echo pulse activated… Echo pulse activated…"

An elderly figure appeared, coming towards them in the gloom. His white hair was parted in the middle of his rather large head. He was wearing a long cloak, but as he approached there didn't seem to be any sign of his legs moving underneath it. He pulled out a signal display unit and, after he had pushed a few buttons, the beeping and the mechanised voice fell silent. He turned and folded his arms.

"Oh dear. Visitors," he sighed. He looked at the silver orb that was gently quivering by now.

"You've got a malfunction. Off you go to maintenance," said the old man.

The orb bumped off into the darkness. Turning to the children he said, "I expect you'll want explanations and everything now."

Sarah and Jack looked at each other. Before Sarah could say anything rude, Jack, pressing his back against the door, said hurriedly, "Well, it's a bit of a shock, of course, but if you don't mind we'll just go home now. We won't say anything to anyone."

"Of course you will – but no one will believe you. Don't worry, you're quite safe," smiled the man. "My name's Zenith by the way and you two are from the twenty-first century. You have found your way into the Planet Earth Humanoid Laboratory. We have other humanoid observatories in different galaxies of course. The silver orbs that seem to puzzle all you humans so much, are a bit like your camcorders, but we call them scopes. Through them, we watch everything you do. We're here to watch all the parallel Earths."

"Parallel Earths?" Sarah muttered, looking a bit stunned.

"Yes," said Zenith. "There are many civilisations all taking place at the same time on this planet. They are all at different stages of technological development. Yours is still in a right mess. You haven't decided yet what to become expert at and you're all fighting each other. One day you'll learn to discuss things reasonably. However, it's still a very interesting piece of research for us."

"What are you talking about?" Sarah snapped, rather offended at being associated with 'a right mess'.

"Let me show you round; you might understand then," Zenith said.

They followed him down a long, twisting corridor. As they went, they passed doors with signs on, like 'Robotic Earth'.

"They've become experts at advanced robotics in that parallel," explained Zenith.

They passed other doors, such as; 'Space Travel Earth', 'Virtual Reality Earth' and 'Microbiology Earth' with Zenith explaining as they went. Eventually they came to a door with a large red cross on it. A sign on the door said 'Clone Earth'. Zenith sighed and shook his head. "This is very sad," he said. "This Earth was doing well, but they took it too far. Oh yes, they got rid of diseases and wars, but there's no longer any development. They all look the same; they all agree. What they need is to start having their own opinions again; think differently from each other. Even their books

say the same thing. There is only one television programme and one film that they watch over and over again. I'm afraid we're going to have to zap it."

"Zap it?" said Jack and Sarah together. "You can't do that!"

"You can go in and see for yourselves if you like. You never know, you might come up with something that will save them," Zenith said. "Don't worry, they'll only think you're ghosts if they see you at all. When you want to come out, simply say so to one of the scopes that we've put in there."

Sarah could sense that Jack would find some reason why they shouldn't go, so she said quickly, "Hurry up and let us in."

"Now look here, Sarah," Jack began, but Zenith had opened the door and with a little push from him, the children found themselves in Clone Earth. They had landed in a classroom. All the children looked exactly the same. Even the teacher looked just like an older version of the children. Everyone was working in total silence. The children were drawing pictures, but every picture was a carbon copy of everyone else's. They were pictures of a garden; all had exactly eleven flowers and two trees. No one seemed to notice Jack and Sarah. Jack sat down on an empty chair and put his head in his hands. He looked very fed up.

"Jack, let's go back to Zenith. We can't let him destroy this Clone Earth or whatever it's called – there's got to be a way to save it." Sarah said.

Jack nodded and went up close to a silver scope that was floating by one of the children. He mumbled, "We'd like to come back now." Instantly, they were in front of Zenith again.

"Well?" the old man said.

Sarah looked thoughtful. "Now look here, Zenith," she began. Jack groaned. "Shut up, Jack. Zenith, we don't know what to do yet, but we want to come back and visit Clone Earth until we find a solution."

Zenith thought for a moment. "Well, it's highly irregular," he mused, "but I don't like zapping Earths. I'll give you until … let's see. It's your summer holidays now, isn't it?" Jack and Sarah nodded. "I'll give you until the end of your autumn half term. That's the best I can do. However, I'll know by looking at the scopes if you tell anyone about all this. Our laboratory will simply find another materialisation spot and I'm afraid you won't have the opportunity to help Clone Earth. I'm sure that won't happen, so, when you want to come back again, just speak to a scope and the laboratory will wait here in the woods for you."

During the weeks that followed, Jack and Sarah visited Clone Earth many times. They went to all its different countries at different times of day and night. Every time they went, Jack and Sarah argued about where to go and what to do. As time went on and they still had no idea how to save Clone Earth, their arguments got worse and worse. They were often seen by people. Many of them didn't believe their eyes and thought they were dreaming. Others thought they were ghosts and would scream and run away. Their one newspaper carried headlines like 'Ghosts Spotted All Over' and 'Dreaming Scientists Study New Phenomena'. However, some would stay and listen to them and a few even joined in with their arguments.

The end of autumn half term came, but Jack and Sarah had not come up with any solution. Although they pleaded in front of the silver scopes that floated in their homes, Planet Earth Humanoid Laboratory no longer materialised in the woods. It seemed they had failed Clone Earth. It was in this mood of despondency that Sarah and Jack were putting up Christmas decorations a month or so later.

"I can't believe Zenith would have destroyed Clone Earth. He couldn't," Jack sighed.

Sarah angrily marched up to a scope that was hovering in her sitting room. "If you're watching, Zenith, I know human life doesn't mean anything to you, does it? We're all just like animals in a zoo, aren't we?" she shouted.

"Oh stop it, Sarah!" Jack snapped.

Sarah was just about to turn on Jack for yet another argument, when she noticed a face appearing in the shining surface of the scope. It was Zenith!

"Ah, Sarah," Zenith said. "Glad to see you're still your argumentative self. I just thought I'd give you an update on Clone Earth."

Jack tried to push Sarah out of the way, but he had to make do with looking over her shoulder.

"Well, there hasn't been a lot of change, I'm afraid," Zenith sighed. The brief fluttering of hope that the children had felt, died. "However, there does seem to be a bit of an interesting problem. It began with the people of Clone Earth discussing whether or not ghosts existed. This developed into heated debates about all sorts of things and now I'm afraid there are outbursts of positive rows going on there. We've decided to give them a few millenniums to see what happens, though with all this quarrelling…"

But Sarah and Jack were jumping around, hugging each other, shouting, "We made them argue! We saved them! Merry Christmas Clone Earth," and they didn't hear another word he said.

Understanding the grammar and punctuation

Nouns and pronouns

Nouns are the names of people, places and things.

Common nouns are names common to all things; for example:

sky, sunset, orb

Proper nouns refer to particular people, places or things. They always have a capital letter; for example:

Sarah, Clone Earth, Wednesday

Pronouns take the place of nouns.

For example:

Sarah saw the sphere and followed it.
('it' refers to the sphere)

Using punctuation to replace intonation and gestures

Colons (:), semicolons (;), ellipses (...) or dashes (–) can indicate a pause when reading.

For example:

Sarah, followed closely by Jack, slipped in behind it: a heavy door silently slid shut behind them.

They were pictures of a garden; all had exactly eleven flowers and two trees.

"I'll give you until ... let's see."

"You're impossible, Sarah – Sarah – wait!"

Ambiguities in sentence contractions

Sentences are sometimes contracted, or shortened, to give impact. This often happens in newspaper headlines and advertisements.

Ambiguities arise when more than one meaning can be understood from what is written. For example:

'Ghosts Spotted All Over'.

This could mean that the ghosts are covered in spots or that people have seen ghosts all over the place.

To make the intended meaning clear – that people have seen ghosts all over the place – some words need to be added:

Ghosts have been spotted all over the place by people.

Nouns and pronouns

Look around you. Write down nine common nouns that you can see.
Write the longest sentence you can think of using all the words.

_____   _____   _____

_____   _____   _____

_____   _____   _____

_____

_____

_____

Read the passage below. Replace some of the nouns with pronouns where you think necessary.

Sarah and Jack met up with Zenith a few years later. Zenith told Sarah and Jack that the people on Clone Earth were still arguing and the people on Clone Earth had begun to write different books and newspapers. Jack and Sarah asked Zenith if Jack and Sarah could read the different books and newspapers to see what the people on Clone Earth were arguing about. Zenith showed Jack and Sarah the different books and newspapers and Jack and Sarah read the different books and newspapers.

The passage below does not make sense! On the back of this sheet, rewrite it so the nouns and pronouns agree with each other and it is clear who or what is referred to. The pronouns that need changing have been underlined.

Jack and Sarah ate some lunch in Robotic World Cafe. Jack had chips which <u>she</u> enjoyed and Sarah had sausages. The sausages were a bit burned, but <u>they</u> was so hungry that <u>he</u> stuffed some down anyway. <u>Your</u> meals were finished off with milk-shakes. <u>It</u> liked <u>it</u> as each one was made with ice cream and strawberries.

Ambiguities and contractions

Many words have more than one meaning – they are
ambiguous. Look at the words below. Insert the meanings in
the appropriate spaces. Use a dictionary to help you.
The first one has been done for you.

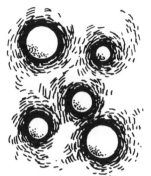

Word	Can mean	Or
Light	Not dark	Not heavy
Arm		
Row		
Wood		
Zip		

Contract the following sentences to make headlines or adverts.

Aliens arrived in our skies to set up an Observation Laboratory.

_____

An amazing polish has been created that will make the silver orb in your house shine.

_____

A visitor from Robotic Earth thought that we all work too hard.

_____

If you want to stop arguing, try drinking 'Quiet Voice' for a relaxing discussion about

your differences of opinion.

_____

Look at these ambiguous contractions. Write two possible meanings for each.
Underline the words or punctuation you have added.

Vampire draws blood – see picture below.

_____

Special offer spectacles for one day only.

_____

Helpful hints for writing a science fiction story

✦ Most science fiction writing is serious in tone, sometimes even frightening.

✦ You might choose to set your science fiction story in a future world, or against the backdrop of an unknown planet. Or you might place your characters in the modern world, but threaten them with alien invasion.

✦ Your story should include some ordinary, recognisable characters with whom the reader can identify. The contrast between these characters and the extraordinary nature of the challenges they face will therefore have more impact.

✦ If you include aliens in your story, be careful when you describe them. Giving an overly far-fetched appearance to them might make them seem comic.

✦ When the characters address one another, they may well refer to some sort of futuristic gadgets.

✦ You should include some of these science fiction plot conventions in your story: time travel; space travel; encounters with alien life-forms; the threat of world domination by hostile alien invaders; and advanced, machine-dependent societies.

✦ Present seemingly incredible events in as plausible a way as possible.

✦ Show the problems faced by people living in the future, or on other planets, and how these problems throw light on, or serve as a warning about, aspects of life in modern society.

✦ Use some techniques to create suspense.

✦ Include descriptions of forms of transport, clothing, food and weapons in future worlds.

✦ In science fiction adventures, the characters usually triumph over the adversity that they face; they overcome the difficulties they encounter.

Science fiction story
Scaffold 1

You are going to write a science fiction story.
To help plan your story, use the framework below.
Choose one option from each stage.

Stage One

Introduce the characters and set the scene.

Two children were at home at the start of the weekend. They had a project to complete for their homework. The project was to design a useful gadget for the future. The children were lazy and were always complaining that they were bored. They were:

a. a boy and a girl;

b. two girls;

c. two boys.

Stage Two

Give the characters a plan/a change/an adventure.

a. They went to the library for ideas for their project. They found a strange book. The book showed how to build weird machines.

b. Their parents, who were scientists and do-it-yourself fanatics, decided to help them with their project.

c. A parcel arrived for them – with strange signs on the box.

Stage Three

Start the characters off on their adventure.

a. The book gave instructions on how to make a travel machine.

b. Their parents decided to make an advanced time and space travel machine out of an old washing machine and bits they found around the house.

c. The box contained different parts of a time and space travel machine and instructions on a video, read by an odd looking person.

Stage Four

Give the characters a problem.

The children made the travel machine and it transported them to a world where gadgets do everything. No one could do anything for themselves. Everyone was lazy and bored.

a. The people on this planet couldn't wash themselves, dress themselves, feed themselves, or do any work because machines did it all for them. Even football matches and other sports were played by gadgets. So everyone just stayed in bed all day. Describe the gadgets and how lazy and bored the people looked and felt in as much detail as possible.

b. At school, the teachers just pressed buttons to get gadgets to give lessons and pressed other buttons to say whether the answers were right or wrong. The children sat in rows pressing buttons all day, while the gadgets did their work for them. Gadgets did games and gym lessons, music lessons and art and drama lessons. Describe these lessons and how lazy and bored the children felt in as much detail as possible.

c. When the people on this planet went on holiday, they were simply transported by travel gadgets. They never did anything on holiday. Even on camping holidays, the gadgets did everything. In as much detail as possible, describe a camping holiday run by gadgets and how lazy and bored the people felt.

Stage Five

The problem is solved.

a. The book the children got from the library also showed them how to make the gadgets not work. The gadgets went crazy and the people had to start doing things for themselves. The characters travelled home.

b. The characters travelled home. They decided to send parcels to the other world containing do-it-yourself manuals and furniture packs.

c. The characters travelled home. They sent the planet camping equipment that could only be put together by the people themselves.

Stage Six

Conclude the story.

a. The characters decided to do more for themselves and never complained about being bored again.

b. The children decided to learn how to do something for themselves, like cooking, sewing or decorating their own bedrooms.

c. The children created a gadget for the school project themselves. It was an alarm clock that runs away and has to be chased to stop it ringing, so getting the children out of bed. They won a prize for this design.

Science fiction story
Vocabulary bank 1

adventure	machines	video
bored	parcel	washing machine
build	parents	weekend
complaining	planet	weird
crazy	project	
design	scientists	
do-it-yourself	signs	
fanatics	space	
gadgets	strange	
ideas	themselves	
instructions	time travel	
lazy	transport	
library	travelling	

My own words

Science fiction story
Scaffold 2

You are going to write a science fiction story.
To help plan your story, use the framework below.
Choose one option from each stage.

Stage One

Introduce the characters and set the scene.

a. Some children were getting ready to go on holiday.

b. Some children who are at boarding-school, were travelling abroad to stay with their parents during the holidays.

c. Some children were late meeting the rest of their class for an educational trip abroad. They caught the next mode of transport out.

Stage Two

Give the characters a plan/a change/an adventure.

Their mode of transport:

a. crashed or sank;

b. was caught in a storm;

c. went into the Bermuda triangle.

Stage Three

Start the characters off on their adventure.

Their mode of transport landed:

a. under the sea in a strange civilisation. Describe this in detail.

b. in an alien dimension. Describe this in detail.

c. on another planet. Describe this in detail.

WHERE SHALL I HAVE THE LANDING?

Stage Four

Give the characters a problem.

The place they landed in was:

a. suffering from pollution. Describe the type of pollution and the effects.

b. suffering from global warming. Describe the effects in detail.

c. suffering from overcrowding. Describe the effects in detail.

Stage Five

The problem is solved.

The children escaped by:

a. hijacking a mode of transport.

b. finding a manual that showed them how to build a mode of transport that would take them out of the place. They built it and escaped.

c. stowing away on a mode of transport.

Stage Six

Conclude the story.

The children learned lessons from their adventures. They:

a. decided to become scientists when they were older so that they could help to prevent the same problem happening on Earth.

b. returned to school and organised a range of activities that heightened awareness of the same problem on Earth.

c. found themselves on holiday where the same problem appeared to be developing. They wrote an article based on their adventures that described what would happen if the problem was not stopped. Newspapers all over the world printed it and governments decided to get together to solve the problem.

Science fiction story
Vocabulary bank 2

abroad
adventure
aliens
article
awareness
Bermuda Triangle
build
caught
civilisation
contraption
crashes
creatures
decide
decision
develop

educational trip
effects
escape
global warming
government
hijacking
holidays
lessons
manual
meeting
mode of transport
organise
overcrowding
planet
pollution

problem
scientists
solve
stormy weather
stow away
strange
together
transportation
travelling
weird

My own words

How Finn became leader of the Fianna

As Finn MacCumhall approached the palace of the High King, he noticed that the road snaking ahead of him shimmered with a magical silver light. It was Hallowe'en, and Finn was on his way to tell the king of Ireland that he wanted to serve him as a member of the Fianna, the special band of warriors that Finn's father had once led.

Finn shivered. Was it because the air was bitterly cold, or was it because this was the night when the doorway opened between the world of the fairies and the world of mortals, and strange events occurred? Kneeling down beside his hound, Bran, Finn buried his face in the dog's warm coat.

"We haven't far to go now, Bran," he murmured. "Look, you can see the lights blazing in the feasting hall."

And, indeed, at that very moment, a magnificent banquet was taking place in the great hall of Tara. Harpists played as the king and his soldiers feasted on roast meats. Jugs of mead and plates piled high with delicious food were passed from man to man. The king had ordered that old grudges should be forgotten, and this company of fierce fighters sat as meekly as lambs.

Boom! Boom! Boom! Who was that knocking on the great oak door?

"Enter!" commanded the king.

Everyone in the hall turned towards the newcomer. He was tall and his back seemed broad enough to carry three men of normal stature. But the most striking thing about the stranger was his hair. It fell to his shoulders and was the colour of a pool of golden sunlight in a forest clearing. At the man's side was an enormous hound.

"My name is Finn MacCumhall," said the young man, kneeling before the king, "and I have come to offer you my service."

Now everyone in the hall turned to look at Goll MacMorna, for it was he who had killed Finn's father. The room was so quiet that you could hear the grass growing in the fields outside the city walls.

"You are welcome," replied the king. "Your father was a great warrior – and he was also one of my closest friends. But I warn you not to seek to avenge his death here tonight. There will be peace among men at this feast."

"I will fight no one here, oh king, only your enemies," promised Finn.

"Then be seated beside my son, Art."

After the meal was over, the men listened to poetry about the great heroes of the past. Finally the king stood up. The light in his eyes had gone out, and all of a sudden he seemed like an old man.

"Friends, for the last nine years on the night of Hallowe'en, Tara has been attacked by a creature from the fairy world, a dragon so terrible that, until now, no soldier has been able to save my palace from it. Unless one of you is willing to stand up to the evil beast, I know that tomorrow morning this magnificent hall will be nothing but … a heap of smouldering ashes. Who amongst you will help me?"

For a moment there was silence. Then Finn rose to his feet and said bravely, "It would be an honour for me to be your champion, oh king. I will protect Tara from this monster."

After he had taken up his sword and shield, he strode out of the great hall, followed by Bran.

"That's the last we'll see of him," whispered Goll MacMorna to his neighbour.

Crunch! Crunch! Crunch! The sound of Finn's footsteps echoed through the darkness as he made his way towards the lonely city walls. Although he could feel his heart pounding inside his chest, Finn was glad that the king had given him the chance to prove himself. It seemed that his whole life had been a sort of preparation for this night, for this fight.

Out of the inky blackness came a voice that startled Finn. He peered into the gloom and was just able to make out a pair of gleaming eyes.

"Finn, before your father died, he saved my life at the battle of Castleknock. Now I want to help you. Take this spear. It is magic and will give you the power to stay awake when the dragon plays its enchanted music of sleep. When Bran barks, place the spear against your forehead. I must go, for I fear the dragon above all things."

Before Finn could thank the man, he had vanished, swallowed up in the murk of the night. Finn scarcely had time to examine the mysterious carvings on the spear before Bran began to bark. (You see, a dog can hear sounds long before a man, and Bran sensed that the unearthly music floating towards Tara over the treetops was dangerous and deadly.)

Bran's barking made Finn realise that he was becoming drowsy, so he quickly did as the stranger had advised him and placed the cold blade of the weapon against his brow. The metal roused him, bringing him to his senses! He felt as though he had just walked through the waterfall in the woods where he had lived as a boy. What a narrow escape! He had nearly fallen under the spell of the dragon's music!

Finn gazed in horrified wonder at the immense creature winging its way towards him. Its cruel, bulging eyes were like red-hot coals. Its once iridescent scales were charred and dull. It carried with it the stench of death. The dragon's wings beat through the air powerfully, fanning the flames of his fiery breath. Each gasp of air taken by Finn scorched his chest. His shield was melting, but the magic spear remained cool. He pressed the blade onto his forehead.

The dragon launched a vast missile of fire on Tara. In a flash, Finn whipped off his cloak, a cloak that had been given to him by his father, and used it to smother the sheet of flame. Fearlessly he leapt on to the dragon's back. The demonic creature screeched in fury and writhed in the air, struggling to shake Finn off. But Finn was too strong for him. He plunged his magic spear into the dragon's shoulder. The creature's death-cry was enough to chill the blood of all honest people from Tara to Dublin. With one blow of his sword, Finn smote the dragon's head from its body. Bran barked triumphantly!

What a commotion there was when Finn presented the High King with the head of the dragon! The Fianna cheered and banged their fists on the table in delight; the harpists played their most uplifting melodies; and the poets put their heads together to compose a poem in honour of Finn.

"Finn, you have saved Tara from the flames of this hideous creature. I owe you a tremendous debt. How can I repay you?" asked the High King.

"By making me leader of the Fianna, as my father would have wished," replied Finn.

"Then so be it. What say you, Goll MacMorna?" MacMorna considered his reply to the king's enquiry carefully.

"I pledge my loyalty to you, Sire, and to the new leader of the Fianna, Finn MacCumhall!" he cried.

That is the legend of how Finn came to lead the Fianna. He proved to be a wise, brave leader, indeed the most famous leader that the Fianna ever had!

Understanding the grammar and punctuation

Different types of sentences

A **simple** sentence has only one clause. This means it has one idea or action and one verb.

The dragon's wings beat through the air powerfully.

A **compound** sentence has two or more clauses usually joined by 'or', 'and', 'but' or 'so'.

The dragon was very big, but it did not frighten Finn.

A **complex** sentence has a **main clause**, which would make sense on its own, and one or more **subordinate clauses**, which depend on the main clause for their meaning.

The dragon's wings beat through the air powerfully, fanning the flames of his fiery breath.

Conjunctions

A conjunction is a word that is used to join sentences or clauses.

Conjunctions include: after, although, and, as, as soon as, because, before, in case, in order to, now, or, since, so, until, when, whenever, where, wherever and while.

Punctuating direct speech

Speech can come at the beginning of a sentence. The words spoken are written inside speech marks. A comma comes directly after the speech before closing the speech marks:

"That's the last we'll see of him," whispered Goll.

Speech can come at the end of a sentence. The speech is introduced by a comma:

Then Finn rose to his feet and said bravely, "It would be an honour for me to be your champion, oh king. I will protect Tara from this monster."

Speech can come at the beginning and end of the sentence:

"My name is Finn MacCumhall," said the young man, kneeling before the king, "and I have come to offer you my service."

Notice that a comma is placed before the speech mark which follows the first part of the speech and again in front of the second part of the speech. The first word of the second part of speech does not have a capital letter.

Complex sentences

Place a comma after the subordinate clauses that begin these
sentences. Then underline the conjunctions.

1   *When Fergus was called to the palace to cut King
    Larry's hair Mrs O'Hanlon began to cry bitterly.*

2   *Although Fergus was frightened he refused to run
    away.*

3   *Before Fergus left for the palace all the villagers
    came to say goodbye to him.*

4   *In order to save her son Mrs O'Hanlon went to beg the king for mercy.*

5   *As he was really a kind man King Larry agreed to the widow's request.*

6   *"Until his dying day Fergus must promise to tell my secret to no living
    thing," the king said solemnly.*

7   *While Fergus was cutting Larry's hair he noticed that the king had
    donkey's ears!*

8   *After returning home from the palace Fergus's life became a misery.*

9   *In order to escape from the village gossips he stayed at home.*

10 *Whenever Fergus tried to sleep pictures of Larry's long, brown, furry ears
    danced before his eyes.*

Now read this paragraph of simple sentences. Choose appropriate conjunctions to join them
together to form compound or complex sentences. Rewrite the text.

*Fergus grew thin. Fergus grew pale. He could not sleep. He could not eat.
Finally his despairing mother went to see a druid. The wise man gave her
some helpful advice. "Fergus should go to the willow tree by the stream. He
should whisper his secret to the tree." Mrs O'Hanlon thanked the druid. Then
she went home.*

_____

_____

_____

_____

_____

Direct speech

Insert speech marks and any other necessary punctuation (capital letters, commas, exclamation marks and question marks) into the following sentences.

1. I need to make a new harp Shane told Fergus.

2. What's wrong with the old one his friend replied.

3. Part of it is broken, and I need to play at the palace ball explained Shane.

4. Fergus thought for a while and then said I saw some fine trees for making a harp by the stream, when I was out walking in the wood the other day.

5. Shane's face broke into a wide smile and he said happily it's great that you're back to your old self: full of bright ideas!

6. Fergus nodded and said it's true that I'm on the mend.

7. I found just what I was looking for said Shane upon his return in the wood by the stream.

8. So laughed Fergus the guests at the party are in for a treat.

9. I hear said Shane that the princess will be there and that King Larry is going to ask her to marry him.

10. Well then said Fergus you'd better start work on the harp straight away!

On the back of this sheet, rewrite the following passage, inserting speech marks, dashes, commas, exclamation marks, question marks and repeated fullstops where necessary, so that the reader can tell the way in which the characters are speaking. A ✦ stands in place of any missing punctuation.

✦Good evening✦ Princess Caitlin. I'm so pleased that you could come to the ball✦✦ said King Larry.

✦I've been looking forward to it✦✦ Caitlin replied graciously.

✦Shane, some music, please✦✦ King Larry called over to his harpist, leading the princess by the hand to her chair.

Shane began to play, and soon the room was filled with beautiful music. It wafted around the banqueting hall like the scent of honeysuckle, enchanting all who heard it.

✦Why, Larry✦✦ said Princess Caitlin✦ ✦you never told me that you had the finest harpist in all of Ireland.✦

✦It's one of my most closely guarded secrets✦✦ said the king sadly.

✦How strange✦ I do believe that the harpist ✦ no, the harp itself is ✦ singing✦✦ whispered the princess in astonishment. ✦Can you hear the words✦ Why, Larry✦ How extraordinary✦✦

Helpful hints for writing an Irish legend

✦ Set your legend against the backdrop of Ancient Ireland.

> *The countryside was lush and green with meadows, mountains, woodland, rivers and lakes. There were small islands near to the beaches and rocky shores of the mainland. The palace of the High King was at Tara. The fairies (the Sidhe) lived in Tir Na n'Og, the Land of Youth.*

✦ Give your characters traditional Irish Gaelic names. Choose names that you know how to spell, as it is difficult for non-gaelic speakers to work out the spelling of Gaelic names from their pronunciation and some of them are accented. For example, the spelling of the name that is pronounced **'Neve'** is **Niamh**.

✦ Your hero should be accomplished not only in fighting skills but also in poetry. He should be intelligent as well as brave.

✦ You might include supernatural characters in your legend, as well as kings and queens, lords and soldiers. Some of the fairies were kind and virtuous; others were spiteful and cast unpleasant spells on those who displeased them. Leprechauns were little people, who were often seen mending a shoe, and who had a hidden pot of gold close by.

✦ One of your heroes or heroines might be changed into an animal or insect such as a deer or butterfly by a character from the fairy world.

✦ Men in Ancient Ireland spent their time hunting, fishing, feasting, reciting poetry and defending their land from attack. They also fought over women. Women in Irish legends are traditionally beautiful and virtuous.

✦ Refer to the music of the harp and the pipes in your story.

✦ Include a battle scene or a struggle between a good character and an evil one in your story.

✦ Be careful not to mention any modern inventions such as television or customs such as 'trick or treat' in your story.

✦ Good usually triumphs over evil at the end of Irish legends, but the good characters sometimes have to endure great suffering. Many Irish legends have a message.

Irish legend
Scaffold 1

You are going to write an Irish legend.
To help plan your legend, use the framework below.
Choose one option from each stage.

Stage One

Introduce the characters and set the scene.

a) Once there were two friends called Shane and Fergus. Shane played the harp at the court of King Larry and Fergus was a barber. They enjoyed fishing and swimming in the countryside around their village.

b) Once there was a widow who lived with her only son, Fergus. Fergus was a good son who had worked hard to look after his mother after the death of his father. He had given up his dream of being a piper to work as a barber, as he could earn more money that way.

c) Once there was a widow who had five children. Her eldest son, Fergus, was a barber, and he gave his mother money to feed his younger brothers and sisters.

Stage Two

Give the characters a plan/a change/an adventure.

King Larry sent for Fergus to trim his hair. For some reason, every barber who cut the king's hair was put to death.

a) Fergus's mother begged him to disguise himself as an old woman and to run away. He refused.

b) Fergus and his friend Shane tried to think of a plan to save Fergus, but they couldn't!

c) All of the people in the village came to say goodbye to Fergus. They were sure that he would not return alive from the court of King Larry!

Fergus's mother went to see King Larry to beg him not to kill her son. The king said that Fergus could live, as long as he promised not to tell the king's secret to any human being.

Stage Three

Start the characters off on their adventure.

When Fergus started to cut the king's hair, he saw that Larry:

a) had the ears of a donkey! Fergus was so surprised that he snipped his own finger with the scissors;

Continued on next sheet.

Continued from previous sheet.

b) had the ears of a horse! Fergus realised that this was the reason why the king had chosen such a strange hairstyle!

c) had the ears of a mule! Fergus shivered but pretended not to notice.

Stage Four

Give the characters a problem.

a) Everyone in the village asked Fergus about his visit to the king, but Fergus would not tell King Larry's secret to anyone. He grew thin and pale.

b) Fergus had dreams about King Larry's ears every night. He found it a great strain to keep the king's secret, and lost his appetite.

c) Fergus could think of nothing except King Larry's secret. In the end he closed his barber's shop and stayed in bed.

Stage Five

The problem is solved.

Fergus's mother asked a wise druid how her son could recover.

a) The druid said that, at midnight, Fergus should tell his secret to the reeds growing under the willow tree by the king's fort.

b) The druid said that, at Hallowe'en, Fergus should tell his secret to the leaves of a willow tree that grew deep in the wood.

c) The druid said that, on May Day, Fergus should climb the willow tree growing by the village stream, and whisper his secret to the bark.

Fergus followed the druid's advice, and immediately began to feel better. After all, he had not told the secret to any human being!

Stage Six

Conclude the story.

King Larry's harpist, Shane, used wood from the willow tree to make a new harp. He started to play the harp at the king's court.

a) Instead of music, a strange wind came from the harp.

b) When Shane started to play, the strangest music came from the harp.

c) When Shane started to play, the voice of the wood-fairy came from the harp.

The wind/music/fairy whispered, "King Larry has the ears of a donkey/horse/mule." No one made fun of the king. He realised that he no longer had to keep his ears a secret! He released all of his barbers, who had not been killed but had in fact been imprisoned in a dungeon!

Irish Legend
Vocabulary bank 1

amazed, astonished,
    astounded,
    flabbergasted,
    stunned
ashamed, mortified
barber
betray
castle
clearing
conceal the truth
court
devise an ingenious
    plan
disappear
druid

embarrassed
escape
farewell
forest
harp
haunted by strange
    dreams
implore
instrument
King Larry wished
    that the earth
    would swallow him
    up!
melody, music
mercy

mysterious
palace
peculiar, unusual
pity
pluck strings
reeds
relieved
responsibility
stream
terrible secret
vanish
widow
willow tree
woods

My own words

Irish legend
Scaffold 2

You are going to write an Irish legend.

To help plan your legend, use the framework below.

Choose one option from each stage.

Stage One

Introduce the characters and set the scene.

It was Hallowe'en. Finn and his dog Bran went to Tara, the home of the High King. The king invited him to join the banquet.

a) Finn had to sit at the same table as the man who had killed his father. The man's name was Goll MacMorna.

b) The king placed Finn next to his own son, Art.

c) The king said that Finn's father had been a great friend of his.

Stage Two

Give the characters a plan/a change/an adventure.

a) The king said that, for the past nine years, Tara had been attacked at Hallowe'en by a fire-breathing dragon. He asked if anyone at the banquet would try to kill the creature. Finn said that he would fight the dragon.

b) The king said that, every Hallowe'en, a wicked goblin called Aillen attacked Tara. Each year he would burn the castle to the ground with his fiery breath. Finn said that he would guard the castle.

c) The king said that, every Hallowe'en for nine years the grandson of the Lord of the Underworld had attacked Tara with fire. Finn said that he would guard the castle.

Stage Three

Start the characters off on their adventure.

a) Finn walked to the walls of Tara. A stranger, who had been helped by Finn's father, gave him a magic spear to help him defeat the dragon.

b) Finn and Bran went to the city walls. Finn took with him a bag of treasure that had belonged to his father.

c) Finn went to the city walls. On the way he met an old friend, who was a robber. The robber gave Finn a magic spear. (It had once belonged to Aillen himself!)

Stage Four

Give the characters a problem.

As the dragon/Aillen came towards Tara, he played magical music from the Fairyworld. This music was supposed to make everyone fall asleep so that Tara was left unguarded. Bran gave a bark to warn Finn of danger.

a) Finn put the magic spear to his forehead.

b) Finn took a magic hat from his father's bag of treasure. He pulled it down over his ears.

The spear/cap stopped Finn falling asleep so that he was able to stay awake to fight the dragon/Aillen.

Stage Five

The problem is solved.

a) Finn threw the spear at the dragon, which fell down dead. Finn cut off the dragon's head.

b) Finn took a magic spear from the bag of treasure. Fire could not burn it. He threw it at the dragon/Aillen. The dragon/Aillen disappeared, never to be seen again.

c) Aillen tried to run away from Finn, but Finn caught up with him and threw the spear at him and he was killed. Finn cut off Aillen's head.

Stage Six

Conclude the story.

a) The High King gave Finn a wish. Finn said that he would like to become leader of the Fianna.

b) The High King made Finn leader of the Fianna. Goll MacMorna agreed to serve him faithfully.

Finn proved to be a wise, brave leader, indeed the most famous leader that the Fianna ever had.

Irish Legend
Vocabulary bank 2

banquet, magnificent feast

brave, valiant

defend, guard against attack

devastation, in ruins

display of great courage

eloquent poet

fair, flaxen-haired, golden-haired

faithful companion

fall into a deep sleep, slumber

feast on wild boar

fire, blaze, burst into flames, clouds of dense black smoke and ashes

harpist

honourable, noble

leader, inspired loyalty and devotion from his men

magical, supernatural

make merry, cheerful, in good spirits

mesmerising music

Samhain (Hallowe'en)

serious, solemn

serve the king

sever the creature's head

slay

terrifying, monstrous

triumph

wicked, fiendish

wide awake, alert

wise, full of insight

My own words

Sedna

In the icy wastelands of the Arctic Circle live a race of people called the Inuit. As whales, seals, fish and caribou used to be abundant long ago in the area where they lived, the Inuit would hunt for these creatures in all seasons. Forests grew around the coasts and the Inuit used the wood for fuel and to make tools. The wood was also used to make small one-person boats called kayaks or larger boats called umiaks. These boats were framed with wood and covered with sealskin. The Inuit made their clothes from seal and caribou pelts. If the weather was mild, they lived in tents made out of animal skins. When the dark, harsh winters sent screaming, endless winds rushing across the Arctic plains, the Inuit made earth huts with roofs supported by whale ribs and shoulder blades. When they were on the move hunting, the Inuit made snow houses, called igloos, shaped from blocks of hard snow.

The Inuit lived together in groups that used a common hunting ground, usually near a large bay along the coast. In one of these groups lived a beautiful girl, called Sedna. Sedna had hair as black as sealskin and as shiny as the ice that glinted under the dark night sky. Her hair fell in silky waves to her knees. Sedna's eyes were large and black, but like coals on a fire, they could glow softly or suddenly spark and flash with flames of anger. Sedna was tall and she moved like a shadow of a cloud across the snow, in her soft sealskin dress.

Sedna spent all her time looking after the dogs that pulled the sledges, training them and talking to them. Since Sedna loved the dogs, they followed her wherever she went. With the people in her tribe it was a different matter. With them, Sedna was cold and haughty. All the young men in Sedna's tribal group were in love with her. Whenever her tribe met another, all the young men in that group fell in love with her too. Soon, Sedna's name was whispered with longing throughout the tundra, forests and icepacks of the Inuit hunting grounds. Every day a young Inuit would ask Sedna to marry him.

Every day Sedna scornfully refused and returned to her beloved dogs. Rejected, the young men would sit around their smoky fires at night, listening to the howling of the wolves and muttering that Sedna would rather be married to her dogs than to any strong and handsome Inuit male like themselves.

One day, it so happened that many Inuit groups had met together by a large bay to hunt the massive bowhead whales that had been seen there.

That night, a group of young men told each other about their love for Sedna. As they spoke, they grew more and more angry about how she had rejected them.

"How can she love those dogs more than me?" each one cried. "It isn't normal. She must be bewitched or cursed and it will bring bad luck on all our tribes."

As the night wore on, the young men decided that if they couldn't marry Sedna, then no one was going to. They agreed that they had no choice but to kill her to save their tribes from the misfortune Sedna's strange love for her dogs would bring.

The following day, when the hunters were busy getting ready for the hunt and the dogs had been tied up, the group of young Inuit went looking for Sedna. They found her sitting alone by the stony shore. Before she could ask them what they wanted, they grabbed hold of her and wrapped a strip of sealskin across her mouth. Carrying her as she struggled, they threw her into an umiak, climbed in and pushed out onto the cold, grey sea. A cutting wind threw snow and ice into their stinging faces as they paddled. When they had gone far enough for no one on shore to see them, they lifted Sedna up and threw her overboard. But as she went over the edge, Sedna grabbed hold of the frozen side of the boat and clung on as the umiak rolled and dipped on the heaving waves.

The young men tried as hard as they could to prize Sedna's fingers from the ice-rimmed umiak, but her fingers had stuck fast to the frozen edge. Sedna stared at them in horror as she saw one of the young men pick up an axe. Egged on by the others, the young man chopped off the fingers of Sedna's right hand. Sedna screamed under her sealskin gag, tossing her head right and left in agony. Her long black hair, now soaked with seawater and blood, whipped across the shouting faces leaning over the edge of the umiak. Yelling at Sedna to let go, the young men pulled her hair away from their eyes. As they peered down at Sedna, they saw her fingers floating on the choppy waves. The fingers grew larger and larger and the fingers grew darker and darker.

Suddenly, the fingers, one by one, swooped under the surface of the water, turned into seals and darted, twisting and turning away into the ocean.

The young men hit out at Sedna who was still stuck by her left hand to the side of the umiak.

"We knew you were bewitched and bad luck. Get off; get away from us," they howled.

Lifting the axe again, they chopped off the fingers of Sedna's left hand. As the fingers fell into the sea, they turned into walruses, whales and dolphins that leaped and dived and sped away. Sedna, with a last anguished look at the wide white sky above the sea, sank to the ocean floor and became a spirit. In the dim, green, echoing water, Sedna's fingers, now all sea creatures, gathered round her. Her beautiful long black hair streamed like seaweed through the ocean and along the sandy floor. Sedna stood up, swaying with the currents that eddied back and forth. Blood from the stumps where her fingers had been, streaked away in thin wisps until the cold of the water froze the raw flesh. Sedna let out a long low moan that travelled on and on across all the oceans of the world.

Every sea creature heard the sound and came teeming to where Sedna stood. Her dogs on land heard it too. The fur on the back of their necks rose and they stood staring out to sea, baring their teeth and growling ferociously. They saw the young men returning and getting closer to the shore, their faces white with shock. The dogs, smelling Sedna's blood on the axe and with an instinct born out of their love for Sedna, tore onto the umiak and in a fury ripped the life out of the young men with their teeth. Jumping into the water, the dogs swam to Sedna's side under the sea.

As time went on, Sedna became the Queen of the Underworld and mistress of all living things. She never forgot the cruelty she suffered and her dark eyes flashed with torment and rage at the slightest thing. Every time someone above the sea did something wrong, the sin sank down into the ocean and got caught in Sedna's hair. As she had no fingers, she could not clean it, brush it or dress it. Her once beautiful hair became tangled, filthy and glued with all the evils of the world. Sedna was enraged. She shut away all creatures. No one could fish or hunt.

The Inuit said that the only way to placate Sedna was for someone to travel down to her under the sea. This person had to be a brave, holy person who could talk to spirits. The Inuit call these people shamans. The shaman would have to pass the huge, fierce and faithful dogs that guarded her. The holy person then had to comb out all the sticky sins and bathe Sedna's tangled hair until it was soft and gleaming again. The shaman made two thick plaits for Sedna so that her hair did not float up to the surface and get caught in the fishing nets. As the holy person gently washed and dressed Sedna's hair, she slowly calmed down and relaxed. When the shaman had finished, Sedna was so grateful she freed all the creatures so that humans could hunt, clothe, shelter and feed themselves again.

Sedna is the most important spirit for the Inuit people because she rules whether they live or die.

Understanding the grammar and punctuation

Making sentences in different ways

You can change sentences by:

a: Combining two or more sentences by adding conjunctions. For example:

Sedna was tall. She moved like a shadow.

could become:

Sedna was tall and she moved like a shadow.

b: Reordering the clauses in a sentence. For example:

They lived in tents made out of animal skins if the weather was mild.

could become:

If the weather was mild, they lived in tents made out of animal skins.

c: Taking words away or changing the words you use. For example:

Sedna had hair as black as sealskin and as shiny as the ice that glinted under the dark night sky.

could be shortened to:

Sedna had black hair.

d: Making the sentence very short. For example:

Sedna was enraged. She shut away all creatures. No one could fish or hunt.

Using commas

If a subordinate clause starts a sentence, a comma is put at the end of the clause.

For example:

If the weather was mild, they lived in tents made out of animal skins.

Here are some conjunctions that can start a subordinate clause. If these words start a clause at the beginning of a sentence, you add a comma at the end of the clause:

while, when, although, if, since, before, as, unless, though

For example:

Since Sedna loved the dogs, they followed her wherever she went.

Changing sentences

Turn these simple sentences into compound sentences by adding 'or', 'but' or 'and' to them. You may have to delete one or more words when you join them:

1. *She must be bewitched. She must be cursed.*

    _____

2. *Sedna's eyes were large. Sedna's eyes were black.*

    _____

3. *Sedna was tall. She moved like a shadow.*

    _____

4. *Sedna loved the dogs. Sedna did not like people.*

    _____

5. *They tried to prize Sedna's fingers from the umiak. Her fingers had stuck fast.*

    _____

Write a subordinate clause to go at the beginning of these sentences, using conjunctions such as : when, if, although, since, while, unless, as, before. Remember to put a comma after the subordinate clause that starts the sentence.

1. *They lived in tents made out of animal skins.*

    _____

2. *Sedna always refused to marry them.*

    _____

3. *They wouldn't have agreed to kill her.*

    _____

On the back of this page, rewrite the paragraph below using as few words as possible, making sure it still makes sense. Can you do it in fewer words than everyone else?

Her beautiful long black hair streamed like seaweed through the ocean and along the sandy floor. Sedna stood up, swaying with the currents that eddied back and forth. Blood from the stumps where her fingers had been, streaked away in thin wisps until the cold of the water froze the raw flesh. Sedna let out a long low moan that travelled on and on across all the oceans of the world.

Using commas

Charlie has rewritten the myth of Sedna.
He has missed out the commas. Put them in for him.

Once upon a time there was a girl called Sedna. She had long black hair and lived in the Arctic Circle with her tribe called the Inuit. The Inuit hunted lots of animals including whales seals and caribou. They moved about so that they could follow these animals which were important to their lives because they used them for food shelter clothing and tools. Every boy loved Sedna but she only loved her dogs so the boys got mad and killed her by chopping off her fingers as she clung to a boat. Her fingers turned into sea creatures. Sedna became Queen of the Underworld but because sins got caught in her hair and she remembered how cruel the boys had been she sometimes made all the animals disappear. So someone had to go and make her hair clean like shiny sealskin before she would let the animals come back to be hunted.

Turn these sentences into complex sentences by adding the subordinate clause to the main clause, which is written in bold. You can do this by using commas or adding a conjunction or both.

1. **The Inuit made snow houses.** *They were on the move hunting.*

_____

2. **Sedna was cold and haughty.** *With them.*

_____

3. **Sedna stood up.** *Swaying with the currents that eddied back and forth.*

_____

Helpful hints for writing an Inuit myth

✦ Most myths are told using a third person narrator.

✦ The setting of your story should be the mythical world in which the Inuit believe. The environment is very important – the Inuit believe the land and snow 'speak' to them. The family is also very important to them.

✦ If you are retelling an Inuit myth, it is important to keep the facts the same when you are writing it:
– Keep the names of the characters the same.
– Keep the places and names of the culture the same.
– Keep the basic storyline the same.

✦ After you have kept all these the same, you can use your imagination to fill in descriptions of places, feelings, people and events.

✦ Myths were told to explain things that people didn't always understand. These things were to do with the natural world; for example, why the sun rises. They were also told to explain things about our lives and deaths.

✦ When you rewrite a myth, it is important that you understand what the myth is going to explain. In the case of Sedna it explains why the hunting was sometimes bad. In scaffold 1, the myth explains how people thought of the hugeness of the world. In scaffold 2, the myth explains natural disasters like earthquakes and the importance of fine words and music in creating a peaceful and safe world.

✦ Try to make it clear to the reader what the myth is trying to explain.

✦ Although you can write dialogue for the characters in myths, a lot of what they say is written through reported speech. That is, the writer acts like a reporter telling the reader what was said, rather than the characters doing the talking.

✦ At the end of the myth, you can add a small paragraph telling the reader a little bit about how the people who created the story feel about the main character in the myth. Or you could say a little bit about the meaning or explanation in the myth.

✦ Myths are often about gods and goddesses. They often have fantastic creatures in them or amazing events that wouldn't normally happen.

Inuit myth
Scaffold 1

You are going to write a traditional Inuit myth.
To help plan your story, use the framework below.
Choose one option from each stage or two if the stage is in sections.

Stage One

Introduce the characters and set the scene.

Once there were:

a) Two men.   b) Two women.

c) Two married couples.

They lived in the Arctic Circle. They fell to talking.
They said:

a) "The world is too big to travel round."

b) "I wonder how big the world is."

c) "The world is never ending."

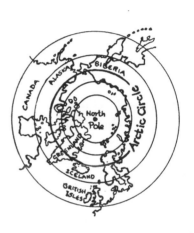

Stage Two

Give the characters a plan/a change/an adventure.

They decided to find out about the size of the world by travelling in opposite directions. They:

a) packed up and travelled by sledges pulled by many dogs;

b) packed up and began to walk across the icy land;

c) packed up and rode on ponies.

Stage Three

Start the characters off on their adventures.

Year after year they travelled. They had many adventures. They:

a) met fierce animals like polar bears;

b) travelled across cold and hot lands and oceans;

c) learned new customs everywhere they went.

Stage Four

Give the characters a problem.

The characters grew very old. Their dogs or ponies died from exhaustion and old age or they could no longer walk. They managed to keep on travelling by:

a) getting new ponies;

b) getting new dogs;

c) getting some people who were also travelling to help them.

But they knew that these dogs / ponies / people would grow tired and old too.

WHICH PROBLEM SHALL I GIVE THEM?

Stage Five

The problem is solved.

Just as they were all on their last legs, they saw:

a) the other characters coming towards them;

b) the place they had started from;

c) somewhere they had already passed.

Stage Six

Conclude the story.

The characters were overjoyed and said:

a) "We were right; the world is very big and full of surprises."

b) "The world is much bigger than we thought and we are glad to be home."

c) "The world is big, but it is not never-ending. It's round."

The characters learned that there is more to the world than one's own environment.

WHICH ENDING SHALL I CHOOSE?

Inuit myth
Vocabulary bank 1

ancient

blizzard

bundle

circumnavigate

colossal

delighted

depart

dimension

elated

elderly

enormous

glacier

glide

huge

huskies

icicles

igloo

immense

Inuit

load

massive

North Pole

ripe old age

savage

sledging

slide

snow-capped

snowdrift

snowshoes

snowstorm

tramp

travelling

trek

vast

wander

My own words

Inuit myth
Scaffold 2

You are going to write a traditional Inuit myth.
To help plan your story, use the framework below.
Choose one option from each stage, or two if the stage is in sections.

Stage One

Introduce the characters and set the scene.

The Inuit people live in the frozen lands of the Arctic Circle.
When the world was first born:

a) there was no light.   b) it was always night time.

c) the sun stayed away from the icy lands of the Inuit people.

During this time there lived a crow and:

a) a chief and his daughter and grandson.

b) a grandmother, her daughter and grandchild.

c) a family with a small child.

WHICH CHARACTERS SHALL I CHOOSE?

Stage Two

Give the characters a plan/a change/an adventure.

The crow told the Inuit people he had seen sunlight on his journeys.
The Inuit wanted to get hold of this daylight because:

a) they could hunt further afield.

b) they could hunt for longer.

c) they could see polar bears coming and run before they were attacked.

Stage Three

Start the characters off on their adventure.

The Inuit begged the crow to go and bring them back some sunlight.
At first he refused because it was to be found a long way away and
he was old. The Inuit begged him and at last he agreed. He:

a) flew into the dark sky towards the east.

b) flew for a long time until his wings were tired.

c) flew on and on until he saw a dim glow of sunlight.

He arrived where the whole sky was bright and he could see for miles.
He landed on a tree near a village. It was still very cold.

Stage Four

Give the characters a problem.

The crow saw a family with a child who had balls of sunlight in a box, but:

a) the box was guarded by the chief/grandmother/head of the family.

b) the family wouldn't want a crow inside their snowlodge and they might shoot him.

c) the crow was too scared to go and ask for the sun balls.

Stage Five

The problem is solved.

The crow changed himself into a speck of dust and floated down. The speck of dust floated:

a) into the child's ear.　　b) up the child's nose.　　c) into the child's eye.

The child began to cry. The family wanted the child to be happy so they put some string round a ball of sunlight and went outside to play in the snow. The dust fell out and:

a) suddenly changed back into the crow which frightened the family. They dropped the ball of sunlight. The crow picked it up and flew off.

b) the dust changed back into the crow, who put out his claws, grasped the string and flew off with the sun ball.

c) the dust changed back into the crow who looked so old and cold that the family gave the sun ball to him to warm him up.

Stage Six

Conclude the story.

The crow took the ball of sunlight back to the Inuit people. He let go of the string and the ball dropped to the ground and shattered into tiny pieces. Light went into every home and darkness left the sky. The Inuit were delighted. They said:

a) 'We can see for miles.'

b) 'Look how blue the sky is.'

c) 'It feels so much warmer now.'

The crow told them it was only one ball of sunlight and was only enough for half a year's daylight. The Inuit said:

a) 'Half a year is better than none.'

b) 'We're still happy and will always be grateful to you.'

c) 'We will always take care of you – in case you take our sunlight back.'

Myth
Vocabulary bank 2

aggression

ancient

bleak

burnish

celestial

charge, rush

cosmos

creation

dazzle

drift

extreme

feeble

glacial

glimmer

glisten

gloom

illuminate

luminescent

lustrous

nocturnal

onslaught

pitch-dark

prolong

protract

remote

shadow

shrivelled

subzero

twilight

universe

waft

wander

withered

My own words

Sarvar and his stepbrothers

A long time ago in India, there was a young man called Sarvar who lived on a tiny farm where nothing much ever grew. Despite being poor, Sarvar was cheerful, contented, kind and generous. His three stepbrothers, on the other hand, were the opposite. They were nasty, mean and spiteful but, because he was the kind of person who would never think badly of anyone else, Sarvar loved them.

The three stepbrothers didn't like Sarvar at all – his generosity and good spirits made them angry and jealous. One day, Sarvar was told that he had inherited (from his grandfather who had died) a rich, fertile piece of land on which to farm. Sarvar was saddened by his grandfather's death but grateful for his inheritance.

"Come and share my land," he kindly invited his stepbrothers. The stepbrothers rubbed their hands greedily, only too willing to take some of Sarvar's good fortune.

When they saw the land, the stepbrothers took the best pieces for themselves, leaving Sarvar with only a small, dry, rocky patch of ground. Still, Sarvar didn't complain. Instead, he rose each morning, giving thanks for what he had and set out cheerfully to do his work. The three stepbrothers sniggered as they watched Sarvar working hard on the dry land.

"It would take a miracle for anything other than weeds to grow on that!" they jeered.

However, a miracle is exactly what happened. At harvest-time, Sarvar's crop was ten times bigger than that of his stepbrothers. They were astounded by what they saw! Sarvar was concerned about their lack of good fortune.

"Take whatever you need from my store," he offered.

Without hesitation, the jealous brothers took everything – all but one sack of grain. Despite their greed, Sarvar did not complain. He gave away the last sack of grain to feed the poor and the sick, living off the last few scraps he could find. Strangely, although he had little left, Sarvar was happier than when his storehouse was bursting with grain.

Soon afterwards, Sarvar and his stepbrothers were called by the District Governor to the city to pay taxes on their land. The mean stepbrothers had no intention of paying their share of the bill. Instead, they formulated a wicked plan to trick Sarvar. They told him that they were taking a trip to the city and asked him if he would like to join them. Sarvar accepted with his usual happy smile and the four men set off.

As soon as they reached the city, the brothers turned to Sarvar and said, "Don't forget to pay your taxes, Sarvar. We only help on **your** land so don't expect **us** to pay!"

Rather than being angry with his stepbrothers for their unkindness, Sarvar was concerned about embarrassing them because – having given away all of his wealth – he had nothing left to pay the bill. Sarvar fell to his knees in the middle of the square and began to pray that he wouldn't bring shame on his family. Passers-by stopped and stared, curious about this strange man and, by the time the District Governor arrived, a huge crowd had gathered.

The District Governor decided to find out whether Sarvar was as holy as he seemed. Holy men were usually offered food and drink so the District Governor told a guard to take Sarvar a tray upon which he placed a bowl and jug, covered with a cloth. He would soon discover whether Sarvar had miraculous powers as the bowl and jug were empty! The guard handed Sarvar the tray and was astonished when, after Sarvar had blessed the tray and removed the cloth, he saw the bowl was filled with rice and the jug overflowed with milk. Hearing this news, the District Governor sent for Sarvar.

When the three stepbrothers saw Sarvar being taken away, they leapt for joy, shouting, "At last, Sarvar is in trouble!"

How wrong they were. The District Governor gave Sarvar gifts of gold coins, a beautiful robe and a fine horse. The jealous stepbrothers were speechless. They plotted to kill Sarvar and steal his riches. However, the District Governor heard about their plan and had them thrown into jail.

Even after their plot to kill him, Sarvar forgave his stepbrothers and asked that they and the other prisoners be released. The District Governor agreed. The other criminals were so grateful to Sarvar that they vowed to follow his example and live good and honest lives.

Sarvar was saddened by the poverty and sickness he saw in the city. Without a second thought, he gave away his expensive gifts to help the poor and needy. Once again, his stepbrothers saw a way to ruin Sarvar's reputation once and for all. They went straight to the District Governor and told him that Sarvar had deliberately insulted him by giving away his gifts.

How foolish they looked when Sarvar came riding through the streets on the fine horse, wearing the beautiful robe and carrying the sacks of gold coins. Even though Sarvar had never felt comfortable with such riches, he had been rewarded again by God for his kindness and unselfish deeds. From that moment on, Sarvar was always able to help those in need. And his stepbrothers? They had their just rewards by staying poor and unhappy for the rest of their lives.

Understanding the grammar and punctuation

Prepositions

A preposition is a word like *on, at, over, by* or *after* which is usually followed by a noun phrase.

A long time ago in India, there was a young man called Sarvar who lived on a tiny farm where nothing much ever grew.

Prepositions can be used to show:
time: ***from*** *that moment on*
position: ***in*** *the city*
direction: ***through*** *the streets*
possession: *the land had belonged* ***to*** *his grandfather*

Some common prepositions include:

in, during, behind, by, over, with, at, on, before, throughout, since, inside, of, along, to, across, between, after

Dashes

A dash can be used to show a pause.

The three brothers didn't like Sarvar at all – his generosity and good spirits made them angry and jealous.

Brackets

Brackets can be used to provide the reader with extra information.

One day, Sarvar was told that he had inherited (from his grandfather who had died) a rich, fertile piece of land on which to farm.

Prepositions

Choose prepositions from those below to complete the passage.

of	about	without	at	in	by	after	to	when
over	before	beneath	between	until	with	on

Sarvar lived _____ India. _____ his grandfather left him some farming land, he decided to share the crop grown _____ it _____ his stepbrothers. His stepbrothers were very lazy, however, and did not help _____ or _____ the harvest. Instead they slept _____ the cool trees or went visiting their friends _____ the crop was ready.

Read these sentences. Decide whether the underlined prepositions indicate time, position, direction or possession. Write 'time', 'position', 'direction' or 'possession' after each example.

1. <u>At</u> harvest-time, Sarvar's crop was ten times bigger than that of his stepbrothers.

   _____

2. How foolish they looked when Sarvar came riding <u>through</u> the streets on the fine horse, wearing the beautiful robe and carrying the sacks of coins. _____

3. They told him that they were taking a trip <u>to</u> the city and asked him if he would like to join them. _____

4. Sarvar accepted <u>with</u> his usual happy smile and the four men set off._____

5. Sarvar sat down <u>in</u> the middle of the square._____

6. A guard placed a bowl and jug <u>near</u> Sarvar. _____

7. The guard put a cloth <u>over</u> the bowl and jug._____

8. People stood <u>in front of</u> him to see what had happened._____

9. <u>From</u> that moment on, Sarvar was always able to help those in need. _____

Using dashes and brackets

Dashes and brackets serve the same function – to add extra information that is not essential to the meaning of a sentence. You always use brackets in pairs, but you can use a single dash if the extra information runs to the end of the sentence.

In the following sentences, decide where the non-essential information is and rewrite them using brackets or dashes to separate this from the rest of the sentence, as in the following example:

Without hesitation, the jealous brothers took everything, all but one sack of grain.

Without hesitation, the jealous brothers took everything – all but one sack of grain.

1. *The book, written by an Indian author, is very popular.*

   _____

2. *Year 5 had a great day out. Everyone enjoyed it.*

   _____

3. *Jack, the oldest in the class, celebrated his birthday yesterday.*

   _____

4. *Our teacher is always happy. She sings every morning.*

   _____

5. *In assembly, we were told that our caretaker, Mr Smith, was retiring.*

   _____

6. *The temperature in the hall was stifling, 32°C, this afternoon.*

   _____

7. *Queen Victoria reigned for 64 years, 1837–1901. She was the longest reigning monarch in British history.*

   _____

   _____

8. *My favourite team won the cup. They scored the most goals, 100, this season.*

   _____

9. *Our class, 5X, was awarded the most merits this week. We are the winners.*

   _____

10. *A crowd of people gathered around. They wanted to know what would happen next.*

   _____

Helpful hints for writing an Indian tale

✦ Most Indian tales are based on legends, myths and folklore that took place a long time ago. You can base your own story on a legend, myth, folk-tale or fairy story but remember to retell it in your own way.

✦ It will be easier to write your story if you narrate in the third person and use the past tense. Remember to be consistent with both narrative voice and the tense you use.

✦ In Indian tales there is usually one main character who is good, at least one who is bad and an animal, spirit or deity who helps to win the fight of good over evil. Your main character should find the power or ability to overcome obstacles such as wicked people, famine or poverty.

✦ Your main character will probably be an ordinary person who struggles to make a living from such occupations as farming, fishing or craft-work (such as weaving, rug-making or basket-making). Remember that a lot of children in countries like India do not go to school but work for a living to help their families.

✦ You do not have to give all your characters names. You can refer to them by title (the District Governor), by relationship (the stepbrothers) or by the job they do. If you do give your characters names, make sure they are authentic Indian names like Sarvar,

Sanjeev or Deepak (for males) or Parminder, Meera or Amarjit (for females).

✦ Most Indian tales are based on strong religious, moral or cultural beliefs and many contain an element of the supernatural. Ghosts or spirits in Indian tales can be friendly or harmful and you can use these in your stories but remember to allow good to conquer evil.

✦ In Indian stories, the rich people tend to live in luxurious palaces and large houses and usually have servants. They eat delicious food, wear fine clothing and expensive jewellery. In contrast, the poor live and eat humbly, dress simply and have little to give away.

✦ Remember that India is a hot country and the landscape tends to be dry and dusty. Include in your story descriptions of places, animals, plants, crops and clothing that are distinctly Indian.

✦ Many of the garments worn in India are made from fine fabrics such as silk and are richly coloured. Try to include descriptions of these colours and textures in your writing.

✦ Try to think of the types of dishes that are eaten in India and the spices that are used in Indian cooking. Describe the taste and smell of the food your characters eat.

Indian tale
Scaffold 1

You are going to write an Indian tale.
To help plan your story, use the framework below.
Choose one option from each stage.

Stage One

Introduce the characters and set the scene.

In an Indian village lived:

a. two brothers;

b. two sisters;

c. a brother and sister.

They were very poor. While sibling 1 was happy and content, despite being poor, sibling 2 was miserable and greedy.

Stage Two

Give the characters a plan/a change/an adventure.

One day, the siblings were told that they had inherited a small farm which had rich, fertile land. The farm was a long way from their village so they would have to plan how to get there. They decided to:

a. walk there;

b. cycle there;

c. travel by bus.

Stage Three

Start the characters off on their adventure.

It was very hot and the route they took was hazardous. Some of the dangers they feared along the way were:

a. poisonous snakes;

b. tigers;

c. murderous robbers.

The journey took several days but at last they reached the farm.

Stage Four

Give the characters a problem.

When sibling 2 saw how large the farm was, he/she realised that there would be a lot of work to do. He/she devised a plan to avoid working.

a. He pretended to have been bitten by a snake on the journey.

b. She pretended to have injured herself on the journey.

c. He/she pretended to have contracted an illness from the crowded bus.

This meant that sibling 1 had to do two people's work.

Stage Five

The problem is solved.

At harvest-time, a wise man came to the farm and told the siblings that there would soon be a drought.

a. Sibling 2 was worried that they would starve so he helped with the harvesting.

b. Sibling 2 employed extra helpers to do the work.

c. Sibling 2 bought a machine to do the work so they could both rest.

Soon, they had plenty of food to eat and to sell.

Stage Six

Conclude the story.

a. Sibling 1 gave away most of his wealth to the poor and needy but remained content, happy and healthy.

b. Sibling 2 kept everything for herself and became more greedy, miserable and unhappy.

c. The two siblings agreed to share the work and help the poor and both lived happy lives.

Indian tale
Vocabulary bank 1

bitten	illness	snakes
buffalo	injured	tigers
cycle	journey	travel
decided	land	village
dusty	machine	walk
farm	murderers	work
fertile soil	people	worried
food	poisonous	
happy	poor	
harvest	pretend	
healthy	robbers	
helpers	seeds	

My own words

Indian tale
Scaffold 2

You are going to write an Indian tale.

To help plan your story, use the framework below.

Choose one option from each stage or two if the stage is in sections.

Stage One

Introduce the character and set the scene.

There was once a boy who lived in an Indian fishing village. He was known affectionately as Baba. Baba was:

a. an only child;

b. the only boy of a large family;

c. the youngest child of a large family.

Stage Two

Give the character a plan/a change/an adventure.

Baba was alone one hot day and he was bored. His parents had warned him not to go out into the midday heat because it was very dangerous. Baba ignored their warning.

a. He went to watch the fishing boats bringing in their catch.

b. He went to the shade of the casuarina trees to play.

c. He found a deserted temple.

Stage Three

Start the character off on his adventure.

The sun was high in the sky and Baba soon became very hot and thirsty. He sat down to rest.

Section A: Suddenly, he heard a voice behind him. He looked round and saw:

a. an old fisherman;   b. a boy, about his own age;

c. a girl, about his own age, who was wearing anklets.

Section B: Baba and the stranger soon began a conversation. The stranger told Baba that he/she was waiting for:

a. his fishing boat to arrive;   b. his brothers and sisters;

c. her mother to come back from market.

Stage Four

Give the character a problem.

Section A:

The stranger collected some cowrie shells and asked Baba if he would like to play a game. When the stranger threw the cowrie shells, Baba noticed that:

a. they began to form a word;

b. they began to form a picture;

c. they began to turn red.

Section B:

Baba was afraid and asked what this meant. The mysterious stranger told him that:

a. the word was 'pichilipuiri';

b. the picture was of 'rakshasa', an evil spirit in Hindu mythology;

c. the red was the colour of blood.

Stage Five

The problem is solved.

The stranger asked Baba to takle his/her hand. Just as Baba held out his hand, he heard:

a. his father calling him;

b. his mother calling him;

c. his brothers and sisters calling him.

Stage Six

Conclude the story.

Baba was scolded for going out in the midday heat. He was told that at high noon the spirits of the dead come down to play games with the living and take them away.

a. Baba's father told him that the fisherman had drowned in a storm many years ago;

b. Baba's mother told him that the young boy had been killed while playing with his brothers and sisters;

c. Baba's brothers and sisters told him the story of the young girl who had died on her way to market to meet her mother.

Baba wondered what would have happened if he had taken the stranger's hand. He never ventured out in the midday sun again.

Indian tale
Vocabulary bank 2

alone	family	shimmering heat
anklets	fisherman	spirits
Baba	ignored	stranger
bored	large	tamarind tree
casuarina trees	market	temple
cowrie shells	midday	thirsty
dangerous	mysterious	vanished
deserted	pichilipuiri (ghost)	warning
disappeared	rakshasa (ghost)	
drowned	scolded	

My own words

Story in letters

12 Green Crescent
Newtown

27th April 2003

Dear Emily

Roll on the end of these Easter holidays! My brother's girlfriend is round here **every day** and I have to be quiet because they're revising for their GCSEs. Why can't they revise at her house? You're really lucky, having no brothers or sisters!

I'm really bored without you to go swimming with. I hope you're having fun at your gran's.

Mum says I can have those gorgeous purple sandals I wanted for the summer term. They'll be great if it ever stops raining!
See you soon.

Love

Katie

Orchard Cottage
Borchester

30th April 2003

Dear Katie

Thanks for the letter. It's a bit boring at Gran's, really. The village is miles from town so I can't even go swimming on my own. Gran keeps nagging me to 'entertain yourself' like she did at my age! I think that means playing with sticks and hoops or skipping ropes. Yuck!

Lucky you, getting new sandals. I have to make do with my old Clark's ones from last year. Dad is coming down on Friday night and we'll travel home on Sunday. Can't wait to see you at school next week.

Love

Emily

12 Green Crescent

Newtown

4th May 2003

Dear Emily

What's happening? Jake says he was passing your house on his way to his girlfriend's and there was a 'For Sale' sign in the front garden. You didn't tell me you were moving!

Mrs Harris asked me if you're ill. She needs a note from your dad to say why you're missing school. I've tried ringing your house but there's no reply so I'm sending this to your gran's. I wish she had a phone!

Please write soon and tell me what's going on.

Love

Katie

Orchard Cottage
Borchester

8th May 2003

Dear Katie

It's terrible! My dad's firm want him to go and work in Carmouth so we have to stay at Gran's until the house is sold and Dad can buy one here. I'm cross with him because he didn't say a word about it until Saturday. He said he didn't want to upset me. I have to go to school in Carmouth which means getting up really early because Dad takes me on his way to work and there's loads of traffic. It's SO embarrassing when his rusty old car splutters to a halt outside school!

I hate being the new girl. I had to stand in front of the class on the first day and tell them all about myself. They think I have a strange accent and some of the girls were sniggering. Most of them already go around in groups and they don't seem to want to make friends. And, if that wasn't bad enough, I have to sit next to a really swotty BOY called Tom Bowler! He's shy and hardly says a word and never gets picked for teams in PE. I wish I was back at Newtown Primary!

Promise you'll write to me.

Love

Emily

12 Green Crescent
Newtown

19th May 2003

Dear Emily

School is horrible without you. There was this empty space next to me and, guess what! Mrs Harris has put Jennifer Sowerbutts there. In your place! Mrs Harris said there was no point in Jennifer being on a table by herself when there's room on ours. Oh no! She's so unbearably goody goody and now she's started following me around at playtimes!

Jake's girlfriend has had her belly-button and tongue pierced. I asked my mum if I could have mine done when I'm 16 but she just stared at me as if I was mad. I don't think she approves of Courtney very much.

Anyway, Mum says I can have a sleepover in the summer holidays, so please, please come!

Love

Katie

Orchard Cottage
Borchester

26th May 2003

Dear Katie

I asked my Dad about coming to your sleepover and he looked a bit unhappy. He muttered something about money not growing on trees because I'm already going on an adventure weekend (that Gran's paying for) with school. Maybe he'll change his mind.

I can't believe Mrs Harris put Jennifer next to you! She never says boo to a goose. Tom is quiet, too. I think he's OK really. We have to do a history project (yawn) in groups and it just so happens that he is brilliant at history! The other two in our group are Samantha and Natasha. They're twins and only ever seem to go around with each other. At least **they** speak to me.

Dad's had an offer on the house so we might be able to move out of Gran's soon. I hope so. I have to share a room with her and she snores!

I miss you.

Love

Emily

12 Green Crescent
Newtown

1st July 2003

Dear Emily

I've seen the 'Sold' sign outside your house! Did you know that Mrs Harris's husband comes from Carmouth? She told us today.

I can't believe term is nearly over. Do you know yet if you can come to my sleepover? Jennifer will be coming, too, so I hope you don't mind.

Jake's girlfriend, Courtney, has now dyed her hair pink! Mum nearly had a fit when she saw it.

I was amazed yesterday. We got our reports and mine was 'excellent' for a change. I came 8th in maths. Jennifer, as usual, came 1st but Mum was really pleased with me. Write back soon.

Love

Katie

Orchard Cottage
Borchester

8th July 2003

Dear Katie

At last!! We're moving to Carmouth. The house is about 5 minutes' walk from school. That means Dad doesn't have to drive me there any more! Phew! AND I can go to the leisure centre whenever I want, and pop round to see Tom and the twins who all live nearby! Dad's firm are going to give him a pay rise so he might even be able to buy a new car and Gran is taking me to town after school tomorrow for some sandals as I've finally grown out of my Clark's ones.

The really good news is that we'll be coming to Newtown next weekend to pack everything so Dad says I can definitely come to your sleepover. I can't wait to see you!

I'm glad you have made friends with Jennifer. Dad seems happier now, so who knows, I might even be able to invite you both to stay. I'd like you to meet Tom and the twins. I think you would like them.

See you very soon.

Your friend

Emily

Understanding the grammar and punctuation

Paragraphs

A paragraph is used to link several sentences that all relate to the same topic.

A new paragraph is used each time a new idea, piece of information or the next event occurs in the writing.

Apostrophes for possession

An apostrophe is used to show belonging (possession).
There are three important rules to remember:

1. We use an apostrophe + s for the possessive form; for example:
   my <u>brother's</u> girlfriend
   my <u>Dad's</u> firm
   <u>Gran's</u> house
2. With more than one owner, an apostrophe is added to the end of the word; for example:
   the <u>twins'</u> father
   their <u>parents'</u> house
3. Irregular plurals (for example, men, children) take an apostrophe + s; for example:
   the <u>children's</u> toys
   the <u>men's</u> football team

Two common mistakes are:
1. confusion with *its* (belonging to it) and *it's* (it is/has).
2. confusion of a regular plural form with a possessive apostrophe + s; for example:
   I bought some sweets (not sweet's).
Note: Some other possessive words such as *his, hers, ours, yours or theirs* are not written with an apostrophe.

Using paragraphs

The following letter has not been divided into paragraphs. Using coloured pens or highlighters, mark the text to show the start of a new paragraph for each new idea or piece of information.

Dear Sam

I hope you're enjoying the summer holidays. I'm staying with my grandparents in Wales for six whole weeks because both my mum and dad are busy working. Did you know my mum's job is midwifery? She has to work night shifts so she sleeps during the day. Guess what! Last week, she delivered three sets of twins! It's fun at my grandparents' place. The house is quite big and is surrounded by mountains and lakes. There is a cellar which my sister and I have been making into a huge den. There are loads of things to do outside, too. The garden is huge, with plenty of space for playing football and there's an enormous oak tree with a brilliant tree-house that my dad built years ago. Gran has an organic vegetable garden right at the end and she grows everything you can imagine: carrots, leeks, onions, cabbages, cauliflowers – you name it! Unfortunately, it does mean that we have to eat all our greens but we're always so hungry we don't really mind. Grandad has a computer and he lets me play my games on it, as well as going on the internet. If you send me your email address, we could email each other. My gran wants to know if you'd like to come and stay for a weekend before the end of the holidays. Grandad says he'll take us fishing and camping, if you like. Let me know soon. Have fun!

Jo

Answer Jo's letter to Sam, remembering to begin a new paragraph for each new piece of information.

Apostrophes for possession

Read the following sentences. Each contains one word that needs an apostrophe to indicate possession. Underline the word and place the apostrophe so that the sentence makes sense.
NOTE: be careful – some of the words could be singular or plural. You have to choose which you want them to be!

1. My dads car is very old and rusty.

2. Mrs Harris dog barks very loudly.

3. My brothers friends are playing football in the garden.

4. The childrens clothes are dirty.

5. The twins house is large.

6. The grocers shop advertised potatoes, cauliflowers and apples at reduced prices.

7. Some of the childrens parents helped on the PTA committee.

8. The cat hissed, its back arching as the dogs eyes widened in terror.

9. Mr Smiths garden is tidier than his house.

10. The librarian mended the books covers that had been torn.

Write three sentences of your own that use an apostrophe for possession.

Helpful hints for writing a story in letters

✦ Use likeable first-person narrators. Remember that the reader is seeing the story unfold from **two** points of view.

✦ The letters should be written in a personal, informal style. It is quite acceptable to use slang if this is the way the characters would speak.

✦ Your characters may discuss topical issues in their letters, such as sports, pop stars or current affairs.

✦ Remember to put some humour into the story, even though the characters may have to face some obstacles or problems.

✦ There should be some contrasts or parallels between the two characters and it is important to establish what their relationship is. They may, for example, be schoolfriends, brothers, cousins or pen-friends, or they may share a common interest, such as sports, pets and hobbies.

✦ Try to make the setting as atmospheric as possible. Remember to describe what the characters see, hear, feel, touch etc. Everything needs to be described as vividly as possible.

✦ You can use a combination of literal and figurative language, such as similes, metaphors and idioms, in your story.

✦ You can set your story in the past, present or future. If your story is set in the past, remember to use the language conventions of the time.

✦ Your characters could use email as an alternative to conventional letter-writing.

✦ Try not to let your story drag on for too long. Keep the pace lively by alternating the length of the letters. Your story should come to a satisfactory conclusion. This does not necessarily have to be a happy ending but it should leave the reader with the feeling that the characters have overcome whatever problems or challenges they faced. You can be adventurous with your ending if you wish, using a 'twist in the tale'.

Story in letters
Scaffold 1

You are going to write a story in a letter format.
To help plan your story, use the framework below.
Choose one option from each stage.

Stage One

Introduce the characters and set the scene.

The characters are in the same class at school. They are best friends. They are:

a. a popular child (X) and a shy child (Y);

b. a popular child (X) and a kind child (Y);

c. a popular child (X) and a studious child (Y).

It is the school holidays and the two friends write to each other regularly.

Stage Two

Give the characters a plan/a change/an adventure.

One day, X discovers that his/her parents are moving to:

a. a village in a remote part of the country;

b. a large city, far away;

c. another country.

Stage Three

Start the characters off on their adventure.

Neither of the friends has a telephone so the only way they can communicate is by letter. The new school term begins and X is at his/her new school.

a. X finds it very difficult to settle into the new area because there isn't enough to do and he/she is bored. Y is too shy to make friends with other children in the class and feels lonely.

b. X finds it very difficult to settle into the new area because it is much bigger than the old one and he/she is nervous. Y tries to help X to feel better by telling him/her that everything will be fine.

c. X finds it very difficult to settle into the new country because he/she cannot speak the language. Y promises to help X learn the language.

The friends write to each other regularly, sharing their thoughts and feelings about the new situation and describing what happens to them.

Stage Four

Give the characters a problem.

It is Y's birthday during the next school holidays and he/she is going to have a party.
Y sent X an invitation but it did not arrive.

a. X is upset because he/she thinks that Y doesn't want to be friends any more.
   Y is also upset because he/she is very shy and doesn't make friends easily.

b. X is upset because he/she thinks that Y doesn't want to be friends any more.
   Y is disappointed that X did not answer the invitation.

c. X is upset because he/she thinks that Y doesn't want to be friends any more.
   Y is angry that X did not answer the invitation.

Stage Five

The problem is solved.

a. The invitation was delivered to a different address by accident. X receives the invitation in time to reply to it.

b. The invitation was sent to a different city by accident. X receives the invitation in time to reply to it.

c. The invitation took a long time to reach X. When X eventually receives the invitation, he/she replies with an explanation.

Stage Six

Conclude the story.

a. X's parents agree to take X to the party. X and Y are very happy.

b. X's parents agree to take X to stay with Y for the holidays. X and Y are pleased that X can attend the party.

c. X's parents decide to visit Y's family for the holidays. X and Y are delighted.

Story in letters
Vocabulary bank 1

answer	frightened	nervous
bigger	holidays	parents
birthday	I hope you're having	party
bored	fun	please write soon
brilliant	invitation	school
can't wait to see you	it's terrible here	shy
city	language	speak
country	lonely	travel/ travelling
difficult	make new friends	upset
friend	move/moving	village

My own words

Story in letters
Scaffold 2

You are going to write a story in a letter format.
To help plan your story, use the framework below.
Choose one option from each stage.
Remember to keep the style informal and to use appropriate language.

Stage One

Introduce the characters and set the scene.

The characters live a long way from each other and write to (or email) each other regularly. The characters are:

a. two friends, X and Y. X has moved to a different town or city;

b. two pen-friends, X and Y. X lives on the opposite side of the world. They have never met;

c. two 'virtual' friends, X and Y who email each other. They have never met.

Stage Two

Give the characters a plan/a change/an adventure.

a. The two friends plan to visit each other for a holiday.

b. The two friends plan an exchange visit so they can finally meet each other.

c. The two 'virtual' friends plan to meet each other.

Stage Three

Start the characters off on their adventure.

With only a few weeks until the school holidays, the friends have to decide where and when they are going to meet and ask permission from their parents.

a. X invites Y to come and stay for a week.

b. X's family invite Y to visit for two weeks.

c. X invites Y to visit for a day.

WHICH SHALL I CHOOSE?

Stage Four

Give the characters a problem.

The friends have to agree on the activities they both want to do when they meet.

a. X enjoys spending time in the shopping mall but Y finds that boring and prefers sports. They disagree with each other's suggestions.

b. X wants to spend each day on the beach, swimming and surfing. Y can't swim and is afraid of the water.

c. X wants to take Y around his/her town/city which is full of life, but Y would prefer to stay in, playing computer games.

Stage Five

The problem is solved.

X and Y agree to compromise and to find a range of activities that they would both enjoy.

a. They discuss other pastimes apart from shopping and sports and draw up a list.

b. They discuss other pastimes apart from water activities and draw up a list.

c. They discuss their other hobbies and draw up a list.

Stage Six

Conclude the story.

X and Y are now excited about meeting each other.

a. The friends exchange letters to finalise details of their meeting, with an agreed agenda for their activities, including some time spent on each other's favourite pastimes.

b. The friends exchange letters to finalise details of the holiday with an agreement to spend some time on the beach and some time sightseeing/doing other activities.

c. The friends agree to spend part of the day on activities in X's town/city and part of the day on the computer.

Story in letters
Vocabulary bank 2

activity/activities	friendly	permission
adventurous	friends	quiet/peaceful
anxious	hobby/hobbies	relieved
computer	holiday	scuba diving
details	internet	shopping mall
disagree	meeting	sightseeing
email	noisy	sport
excited	parents	surfing
favourite	pastime	terrified
foreign language	pen-friend	visit

My own words